The Secret Language of Colors

The Secret Language of Colors

Matthew Petchinsky

The Secret Language of Colors: Unlocking the Emotional Codes
By: Matthew Petchinsky

Introduction

The Power of Color: How Colors Influence Our Lives

Colors are an integral part of our world, influencing our emotions, thoughts, and behaviors in ways we often take for granted. From the warm hues of a sunrise to the calming blues of the ocean, the colors around us subtly shape our experiences. They evoke emotions, set moods, and even affect our physical state. Red can energize and ignite passion, while blue soothes and fosters introspection. Green brings a sense of balance and renewal, while yellow sparks joy and optimism.

Throughout history, colors have held profound symbolic meanings in cultures and traditions. Ancient Egyptians revered the color gold as a symbol of divine connection, while in Chinese culture, red is considered the color of luck and prosperity. Beyond symbolism, modern science has confirmed that colors influence us biologically—certain shades can lower heart rates, improve focus, or even stimulate appetite.

Yet, color is more than just a visual experience; it's a language of its own. By learning to interpret and harness this language, we gain the ability to enrich our lives, foster deeper connections with others, and cultivate emotional well-being.

Why Understanding Color Matters in Emotional Well-Being

In our fast-paced, visually saturated world, the significance of color often fades into the background. But what if you could consciously use color to transform your emotions, relationships, and outlook on life? Imagine wearing a particular shade to boost your confidence before an important meeting or decorating your home in tones that promote relaxation and mindfulness. This is the power of intentional interaction with color.

Colors resonate with our emotional and psychological states, making them powerful tools for healing and growth. Therapies like chromotherapy (color therapy) have demonstrated the profound impact color can have on mental health, helping to alleviate anxiety, depression, and stress. Even simple shifts, like surrounding yourself with uplifting colors during challenging times, can have a remarkable effect.

Understanding the emotional language of color equips you with the ability to make deliberate choices that nurture your well-being. By recognizing the impact of your environment, clothing, and even digital spaces, you can create a life that reflects and supports your inner balance.

A Preview of What You'll Learn in This Book

This book, *The Secret Language of Colors: Unlocking the Emotional Codes*, is your comprehensive guide to understanding and utilizing the transformative power of color. Whether you're an artist, designer, healer, or someone seeking personal growth, this journey will open your eyes to the emotional and symbolic dimensions of color. Here's what you can expect:

1. **The Science of Color Perception**: Dive into how our eyes and brain process color, and discover the scientific basis for its emotional effects.
2. **The Emotional Codes of Each Color**: Explore the unique psychological and symbolic meanings of colors across cultures and contexts, including how they influence mood, behavior, and communication.
3. **Harnessing Color in Daily Life**: Learn practical techniques for using color to enhance your surroundings, wardrobe, and even personal branding.
4. **Healing Through Color**: Uncover the principles of color therapy and how specific hues can promote physical and emotional healing.
5. **Building Your Color Blueprint**: Create a personalized plan to align the power of color with your life goals and emotional needs.

Through engaging insights, actionable advice, and inspiring examples, this book will help you unlock the hidden potential of color. By the end of your journey, you'll not only have a deeper appreciation for the vibrancy of life but also a powerful toolset to live with intention, harmony, and emotional clarity.

Let's embark on this colorful journey together.

Part 1: The Fundamentals of Color and Emotion

Chapter 1: What Is Color? The Science Behind the Spectrum

Color is one of the most fascinating aspects of the natural world, a phenomenon that permeates every part of our lives, from the way we perceive the environment to the emotions we feel in response to what we see. But to truly understand the power of color and its impact on our lives, we must first explore what color is from a scientific perspective.

The Nature of Color: A Dance of Light and Perception

At its core, color is not an inherent property of objects but a perception created by the interaction of light with the human eye and brain. When light hits an object, certain wavelengths of the light spectrum are absorbed, while others are reflected. The reflected wavelengths determine the color we perceive.

For instance, a ripe tomato appears red because it reflects light in the red wavelength range while absorbing other wavelengths. Similarly, a clear sky looks blue because molecules in the atmosphere scatter shorter blue wavelengths more than longer red ones. This scattering effect, known as Rayleigh scattering, illustrates how environmental conditions influence color perception.

Color does not exist independently; it is a product of the interaction between three key components:

1. **Light Source**: The type of light illuminating an object (e.g., sunlight, fluorescent bulbs, or LED lights) affects how we perceive its color.
2. **Object Properties**: The material and surface texture of an object influence how it absorbs and reflects light.
3. **Observer's Vision**: The human eye and brain process the incoming light signals to create the sensation of color.

The Electromagnetic Spectrum: Where Color Resides

To grasp the science of color, we must understand the electromagnetic spectrum, a range of electromagnetic waves classified by wavelength and frequency. Visible light, the portion of the spectrum detectable by the human eye, spans wavelengths from approximately 380 to 750 nanometers.

Each color corresponds to a specific range of wavelengths:

- **Violet**: 380–450 nm
- **Blue**: 450–495 nm
- **Green**: 495–570 nm
- **Yellow**: 570–590 nm
- **Orange**: 590–620 nm
- **Red**: 620–750 nm

Beyond the visible spectrum, ultraviolet (shorter wavelengths) and infrared (longer wavelengths) light exist, though they are invisible to the naked eye. However, some animals, such as bees, can see ultraviolet light, and technology like infrared cameras can detect wavelengths humans cannot.

The Human Eye: A Color-Detecting Marvel

The human eye is an intricate organ designed to detect and interpret light. At the back of the eye lies the retina, a thin layer of tissue containing two types of photoreceptor cells: **rods** and **cones**.

- **Rods**: Responsible for vision in low-light conditions, rods are highly sensitive to light but do not detect color.
- **Cones**: Specialized for color vision, cones function in well-lit conditions and are divided into three types based on the wavelengths they are sensitive to:
    - **S-Cones**: Sensitive to short wavelengths (blue).
    - **M-Cones**: Sensitive to medium wavelengths (green).
    - **L-Cones**: Sensitive to long wavelengths (red).

When light enters the eye, cones respond to different wavelengths, sending electrical signals to the brain via the optic nerve. The brain's visual cortex processes these signals, combining information from the cones to produce the perception of color.

The Role of the Brain: Constructing Color

Color perception does not end in the eyes—it is the brain that gives color its meaning. The visual cortex interprets signals from the retina, blending input from the three types of cones to create a full spectrum of colors.

For example:

- Equal stimulation of all three cones results in the perception of white light.
- Stimulation of S-cones and M-cones but not L-cones creates a cyan or bluish-green color.
- Complex interactions between cone types produce intermediate colors and shades.

The brain's interpretation of color is not always perfect. Optical illusions, for instance, can trick the brain into seeing colors that do not exist. Cultural and personal experiences also influence how we interpret colors, making color perception both a physiological and psychological phenomenon.

Beyond Human Vision: Extraordinary Color Perception

While the human eye is remarkable, it is not the pinnacle of color perception. Many animals have more advanced visual systems:

- **Birds and Butterflies**: Possess additional types of cones, allowing them to perceive a broader spectrum of colors, including ultraviolet.
- **Mantis Shrimp**: Known for their extraordinary eyes, mantis shrimp have up to 16 types of photoreceptors, enabling them to detect ultraviolet, infrared, and polarized light.

These differences highlight the subjectivity of color perception—what humans see is just a fraction of the electromagnetic spectrum, shaped by our biology.

The Psychological Effects of Color

The scientific understanding of color extends beyond its physical properties to its psychological effects. Colors influence our emotions and behaviors, often in subtle yet profound ways. For instance:

- Red stimulates energy and passion but can also evoke aggression.
- Blue promotes calmness and trust but can feel cold or detached in excess.
- Green is associated with growth and balance, offering a sense of renewal.

These effects are not universal; cultural contexts and personal associations play a significant role. Understanding the interplay between the science and psychology of color is key to unlocking its full potential in our lives.

Why the Science of Color Matters

By exploring the science behind the spectrum, we gain a deeper appreciation for the colors around us and their impact on our perception and emotions. Color is not merely a visual experience—it is a dynamic interaction between light, the physical world, and our minds. This knowledge empowers us to make intentional choices about the colors we surround ourselves with, using them as tools for expression, healing, and connection.

Chapter 2: Color Perception: How We See and Feel Colors

Color is more than a visual sensation—it is an emotional experience, a biological process, and a psychological phenomenon. Our perception of color is shaped by the interplay of light, the mechanics of our eyes, and the intricate workings of our brain. Furthermore, the way we feel and respond to color is influenced by cultural, personal, and situational factors. In this chapter, we explore the fascinating journey of color from the outside world into our minds and hearts.

The Mechanics of Seeing Color

To understand color perception, we must first revisit the mechanics of how the human visual system processes light and translates it into the vibrant world of colors we experience.

The Journey of Light

Color begins with light. When light from a source (like the sun or a lamp) strikes an object, the object absorbs certain wavelengths and reflects others. These reflected wavelengths travel to our eyes, initiating the process of seeing color.

The human eye, a marvel of evolutionary design, plays a crucial role in this process. Here's how it happens step by step:

1. **Cornea and Lens**: Light enters the eye through the cornea, passes through the pupil, and is focused by the lens onto the retina.
2. **Retina and Photoreceptors**: The retina, located at the back of the eye, contains photoreceptor cells called **rods** and **cones**. Rods handle low-light vision but do not perceive color. Cones, on the other hand, are responsible for detecting color and function optimally in bright light.
3. **Cone Types**: There are three types of cones:
    - **S-Cones**: Sensitive to short wavelengths (blue light).
    - **M-Cones**: Sensitive to medium wavelengths (green light).
    - **L-Cones**: Sensitive to long wavelengths (red light).
4. **Signal Transmission**: When cones detect light, they send signals via the optic nerve to the brain's visual cortex.

The Role of the Brain

Color perception doesn't fully occur in the eyes—it is completed in the brain. The visual cortex processes the signals from cones, combining the input to create the perception of colors. This process is known as **trichromatic color theory**, which explains how the three cone types work together to perceive millions of colors.

In addition, the brain processes color contextually, meaning the surrounding environment, lighting, and prior knowledge influence how we see colors. For instance, the same color can appear different under natural versus artificial lighting—a phenomenon called **color constancy**.

The Emotional Resonance of Colors

While the mechanics of color perception are rooted in biology, our emotional response to colors is shaped by psychology, culture, and personal experiences.

Universal Emotional Effects

Colors evoke certain emotional responses that are consistent across many cultures and individuals:

- **Red**: Associated with energy, passion, and urgency. Red can stimulate the heart rate and evoke feelings of excitement or danger.
- **Blue**: Promotes calmness, trust, and introspection. Blue is often used in environments where relaxation or focus is needed.
- **Green**: Evokes balance, renewal, and a connection to nature. Green has been shown to reduce stress and improve focus.
- **Yellow**: Associated with joy, warmth, and optimism. However, excessive yellow can cause agitation or anxiety.
- **Purple**: Conveys luxury, creativity, and spirituality. Purple is often linked to imagination and introspection.

Cultural Interpretations

The emotional meanings of colors can vary significantly between cultures:

- **Red**: In China, red symbolizes prosperity and good fortune, while in Western cultures, it may signify love or warning.
- **White**: In many Western cultures, white represents purity and new beginnings, but in some Eastern traditions, it is associated with mourning and loss.
- **Black**: Often seen as a symbol of elegance and sophistication in Western fashion, black may represent death or misfortune in other contexts.

Understanding these cultural differences is essential, especially in design, marketing, and communication across diverse audiences.

Personal Influences on Color Perception

Our personal history and experiences play a critical role in how we perceive and feel about colors. These influences include:

- **Memories**: Colors associated with positive or negative memories can evoke corresponding emotions. For example, a person who grew up near the ocean may find blue calming and nostalgic.
- **Personality**: Extroverts may gravitate toward bright, vibrant colors, while introverts may prefer subdued, earthy tones.
- **Mood and Context**: Our emotional state can affect how we perceive colors. A cheerful person might see yellow as uplifting, while someone feeling anxious might find it overwhelming.

The Science of Color and Emotion

Research into the psychology of color has revealed fascinating insights into how colors influence our emotions and behavior:

- **Color Therapy**: Known as chromotherapy, this alternative therapy uses colors to promote healing. For example, green is used to calm anxiety, and orange is believed to stimulate energy and creativity.
- **Marketing and Branding**: Companies use color psychology to influence consumer behavior. Fast food chains often use red and yellow to stimulate appetite, while financial institutions use blue to evoke trust and stability.
- **Interior Design**: Colors are chosen to set the mood of a space. For instance, soft blues and greens are common in bedrooms to promote relaxation, while bright yellows and oranges may be used in kitchens to create energy.

The Science of Color Blindness

Color perception is not universal. Approximately 8% of men and 0.5% of women worldwide experience some form of color blindness, a condition where the ability to distinguish between certain colors is impaired. The most common forms include:

- **Red-Green Color Blindness**: Difficulty distinguishing between reds and greens.
- **Blue-Yellow Color Blindness**: Trouble differentiating between blues and yellows.
- **Total Color Blindness**: Rare cases where individuals see the world only in shades of gray.

Understanding these variations in color perception highlights the diversity of human experiences with color.

The Intersection of Science and Emotion

Color perception is a unique blend of biology and emotion. While the mechanics of color are grounded in the physics of light and the biology of vision, the feelings colors evoke are deeply personal and culturally influenced. This duality makes color a powerful tool for communication, healing, and self-expression.

By understanding how we see and feel colors, we gain the ability to make intentional choices in our environments, wardrobes, and designs to create spaces and experiences that align with our emotional and psychological needs. In the following chapters, we will delve deeper into the emotional codes of individual colors and learn how to harness their power to enrich our lives.

Chapter 3: The Psychology of Color: Emotions and Associations

Color is more than just a visual experience; it is a powerful psychological tool that influences emotions, behavior, and decision-making. Colors can evoke joy, calmness, excitement, or even anxiety, often without us consciously realizing their impact. In this chapter, we will explore the psychology of color, the emotional associations tied to various hues, and how these connections influence our lives and environments.

The Foundations of Color Psychology

The study of color psychology examines how colors affect human emotions and behavior. This field combines insights from science, psychology, and art to reveal how colors communicate nonverbally and evoke emotional responses.

Biological Basis

The human response to color is rooted in biology. Certain colors trigger physiological changes in the body:

- **Red**, for example, can raise heart rates and increase adrenaline production, stimulating a sense of urgency or excitement.
- **Blue**, conversely, has been shown to lower blood pressure and slow heart rates, promoting relaxation and calmness.

These responses are thought to have evolutionary origins. Bright colors like red and orange often signal danger or urgency in nature, while softer colors like blue and green are associated with safe, calm environments.

Psychological Interpretation

Our interpretation of color is not purely biological—it is also shaped by psychological and cultural factors. For instance, while red may universally elicit excitement, its specific meaning varies:

- In Western cultures, it often symbolizes love or danger.
- In Eastern cultures, it is a symbol of prosperity and good fortune.

The psychological effects of color are deeply personal and can vary based on individual experiences and cultural background.

Emotional Associations of Colors

Each color in the spectrum carries its own unique emotional associations. Below is an exploration of the psychological effects of major colors and their common meanings.

Red

- **Emotions**: Passion, energy, love, urgency, aggression.
- **Psychological Effects**: Red is a stimulating color that captures attention and evokes strong emotions. It is associated with both positive feelings (love and passion) and negative feelings (anger and aggression).
- **Uses**: Often used in marketing to create a sense of urgency or excitement and in environments where energy and action are desired.

Blue

- **Emotions**: Calmness, trust, sadness, introspection.
- **Psychological Effects**: Blue has a calming effect on the mind and body, promoting relaxation and focus. However, in excess, it can evoke feelings of sadness or coldness.
- **Uses**: Commonly used in professional settings to convey trust and reliability, as well as in bedrooms and spas for relaxation.

Green

- **Emotions**: Renewal, growth, balance, envy.
- **Psychological Effects**: Green is associated with nature and renewal, creating a sense of balance and harmony. It is also linked to feelings of jealousy or envy in certain contexts.
- **Uses**: Widely used in healthcare, eco-friendly branding, and spaces designed for restoration and calmness.

Yellow

- **Emotions**: Happiness, optimism, warmth, caution.
- **Psychological Effects**: Yellow is a bright, uplifting color that promotes joy and energy. However, it can also be overwhelming in large doses and is associated with caution (e.g., traffic signals).
- **Uses**: Often used in marketing to grab attention and in spaces meant to inspire creativity or cheerfulness.

Orange

- **Emotions**: Enthusiasm, creativity, warmth, appetite.
- **Psychological Effects**: Orange is an energetic and friendly color that stimulates appetite and conversation. It combines the energy of red with the warmth of yellow.
- **Uses**: Popular in food-related industries and in spaces where social interaction is encouraged.

Purple

- **Emotions**: Luxury, creativity, spirituality, mystery.
- **Psychological Effects**: Purple is often associated with royalty, imagination, and spirituality. It can evoke feelings of mystery or introspection.
- **Uses**: Commonly used in branding for luxury goods and in spaces meant to inspire creativity or spiritual reflection.

White

- **Emotions**: Purity, simplicity, cleanliness, emptiness.
- **Psychological Effects**: White is a neutral color that promotes a sense of cleanliness and simplicity. However, it can feel stark or sterile in excess.
- **Uses**: Frequently used in minimalist design, healthcare, and branding for purity or freshness.

Black

- **Emotions**: Power, sophistication, mystery, sadness.
- **Psychological Effects**: Black conveys authority and sophistication but can also evoke feelings of sadness or fear.
- **Uses**: Often used in high-end fashion and branding to communicate elegance or mystery.

The Influence of Culture on Color Psychology

Cultural context plays a significant role in how colors are perceived and interpreted:

- **Red**: In China, red symbolizes good luck and celebration, while in Western cultures, it may signify danger or romance.
- **White**: In Western cultures, white is associated with weddings and purity, but in many Eastern cultures, it represents mourning and loss.
- **Black**: Often a color of mourning in Western cultures, black can symbolize luxury and sophistication in the fashion world.

Understanding these cultural nuances is crucial when using color in global contexts, such as branding, marketing, or design.

The Psychological Impact of Color in Daily Life

In Interiors and Design

Colors in our environment significantly impact our emotions and behaviors:

- **Workspaces**: Blue and green are popular choices for offices as they promote focus and creativity.
- **Bedrooms**: Soft blues, greens, and neutral tones encourage relaxation and restful sleep.
- **Gyms and Fitness Centers**: Bright, energetic colors like red and orange stimulate energy and motivation.

In Fashion

The colors we wear can influence not only how others perceive us but also how we feel:

- **Red**: Worn to make a bold statement or exude confidence.
- **Black**: A classic choice for sophistication and authority.
- **Yellow**: Worn to convey cheerfulness or energy.

In Marketing and Branding

Color psychology is a cornerstone of branding and advertising. Companies carefully select colors to evoke specific emotions and drive consumer behavior:

- **Red and Yellow**: Used by fast-food chains to stimulate appetite and energy.
- **Blue**: Common in tech and finance to communicate trust and professionalism.
- **Green**: Favored by eco-friendly and health-conscious brands.

Emotional Triggers and Personal Associations

While certain colors have universal meanings, individual experiences often shape personal associations with colors. For example:

- A person who associates yellow with a sunny childhood memory may find it uplifting, while another person may find it overwhelming due to its brightness.
- Personal taste and life experiences also influence color preferences, adding a unique layer to how we perceive and respond to colors.

Practical Applications of Color Psychology

Harnessing the psychology of color can have transformative effects on various aspects of life:

1. **Mental Health**: Use calming colors like blue and green in stressful environments to promote relaxation.
2. **Productivity**: Incorporate stimulating colors like yellow in creative spaces or red in gyms to boost energy.
3. **Self-Expression**: Choose clothing or accessories in colors that align with your mood or desired energy for the day.

By intentionally using color, you can create environments, experiences, and expressions that align with your goals and emotional needs.

Conclusion: The Language of Color

Color psychology bridges the gap between science and emotion, revealing how colors communicate with us on a subconscious level. By understanding the emotional associations tied to various colors, we can better harness their power in our personal and professional lives. Whether you're designing a space, choosing an outfit, or building a brand, the psychology of color offers valuable insights to create meaningful and impactful experiences.

Chapter 4: Historical Perspectives: Color Symbolism Across Cultures

Color has played a profound role in human history, serving as a symbolic language that communicates values, beliefs, and emotions. Across centuries and civilizations, colors have carried deep meanings that shaped art, religion, politics, and daily life. This chapter explores the rich tapestry of color symbolism across cultures and historical periods, shedding light on how colors have been perceived, used, and revered around the world.

The Foundations of Color Symbolism

Color symbolism is deeply rooted in the human experience. Early societies often derived their interpretations of colors from their environment:

- **Red**: Associated with fire and blood, often symbolizing life, passion, and danger.
- **Green**: Linked to nature and fertility, representing growth and renewal.
- **Blue**: Associated with the sky and water, symbolizing tranquility and the divine.

These natural associations formed the basis for cultural interpretations of color, which evolved with the rise of religion, art, and politics.

Ancient Civilizations and Color Symbolism

Ancient Egypt

In Ancient Egypt, color was integral to art and spirituality, reflecting the divine and the earthly realms:

- **Gold**: Symbolized the eternal and the divine, often associated with the gods and the afterlife.
- **Green**: Represented fertility and regeneration. Osiris, the god of the afterlife, was often depicted with green skin to signify rebirth.
- **Red**: Represented chaos and destruction but also energy and vitality. The desert was called the "Red Land" (Deshret), contrasting with the fertile "Black Land" (Kemet).

Ancient Greece and Rome

In classical antiquity, color was closely tied to societal values and mythology:

- **White**: Symbolized purity and the divine. In Greek temples, white marble represented the perfection of the gods.
- **Purple**: Associated with wealth and power, as Tyrian purple dye was expensive and reserved for the elite.
- **Black**: Often represented death and the underworld, linked to the god Hades and the concept of mourning.

Ancient China

In Chinese culture, color symbolism was heavily influenced by cosmology and the Five Elements theory:

- **Red**: Symbolized good fortune, joy, and celebration. Red was the color of weddings and festivals.
- **Yellow**: Represented the center of the universe, associated with the emperor and the sun.
- **Black**: Represented water and winter, but also wisdom and depth.

Medieval and Renaissance Europe
The Middle Ages
During the medieval period, color symbolism was intertwined with religion and heraldry:

- **Blue**: Became associated with the Virgin Mary, symbolizing purity and divinity.
- **Green**: Represented fertility and nature but could also signify inconstancy in love.
- **Red**: Symbolized both the blood of Christ (sacrifice) and the flames of Hell (sin).

The Renaissance
The Renaissance brought a revival of classical ideals and a deep appreciation for color in art:

- **Gold**: Represented divine light and heavenly glory, often used in religious paintings to depict halos and sacred imagery.
- **Black**: Signified sophistication and elegance, particularly in fashion among the wealthy.
- **Orange**: Emerged as a color of creativity and vitality, reflecting the humanist focus on life and the arts.

Color Symbolism in Non-Western Cultures

India

In Indian culture, color symbolism is deeply embedded in spirituality and rituals:

- **Red**: Represents purity, marriage, and fertility. Brides often wear red saris during weddings.
- **Saffron**: Sacred in Hinduism, symbolizing renunciation, spirituality, and the pursuit of enlightenment.
- **Blue**: Associated with the god Krishna, symbolizing divine love and compassion.

Africa

African cultures often use color to convey identity, community, and spirituality:

- **Green**: Symbolizes life and prosperity, often tied to the land and agriculture.
- **Black**: Represents unity, ancestral heritage, and the strength of the people.
- **Yellow**: Associated with wealth and status, often seen in ceremonial clothing and jewelry.

Native American Cultures

Colors held sacred meanings in Native American traditions, often varying by tribe:

- **Red**: Represented war and victory but also life and vitality.
- **White**: Symbolized peace and purification.
- **Blue**: Associated with the spirit world and healing.

The Evolution of Color Symbolism in the Modern Era

With the advent of global trade and cultural exchange, the meanings of colors have evolved and often merged across cultures:

- **Purple**: Once reserved for royalty due to its rarity, it is now associated with creativity and individuality.
- **Black**: Transitioned from a color of mourning to a symbol of sophistication in Western fashion.
- **Green**: While still tied to nature, it has become a global symbol of environmentalism and sustainability.

In the modern era, color symbolism continues to play a role in branding, politics, and personal identity:

- **National Flags**: Colors in flags often carry historical and cultural significance. For example, red, white, and blue in the U.S. flag represent valor, purity, and justice.
- **Social Movements**: Colors have become symbols of solidarity, such as pink for breast cancer awareness and rainbow colors for LGBTQ+ pride.

Cross-Cultural Insights into Color Symbolism

While specific interpretations of colors vary, there are universal themes that resonate across cultures:

- **Red**: Energy, life, and passion.
- **Blue**: Peace, divinity, and introspection.
- **Green**: Growth, nature, and renewal.

Understanding these commonalities and differences enriches our appreciation of color as a universal yet culturally distinct language.

Applications of Historical Color Symbolism Today
Art and Design
Historical color symbolism continues to influence modern art and design. Designers and artists often draw on cultural and historical contexts to create work that resonates emotionally with audiences.
Fashion
Fashion frequently revisits historical color meanings. For instance, black remains a staple of sophistication and elegance, while red is often used to make bold, passionate statements.
Marketing and Branding
Brands use historical and cultural color symbolism to communicate their values and appeal to target audiences. For example, green is widely used by eco-conscious brands to signal sustainability.
Conclusion: The Timeless Power of Color Symbolism
The symbolism of color is a timeless, universal language that bridges the past and present. From ancient civilizations to modern societies, colors have shaped how we express identity, communicate values, and connect with the world around us. By understanding the historical and cultural meanings of color, we gain deeper insight into its enduring power to influence emotions, convey messages, and enrich our lives.

Chapter 5: The Language of Color: Universal and Personal Meanings

Color is a language that transcends words, speaking directly to our emotions, memories, and subconscious minds. While certain meanings of color are nearly universal—shaped by natural phenomena, biology, and cultural evolution—others are deeply personal, influenced by individual experiences and associations. This chapter explores how color communicates on both universal and personal levels, and how understanding this duality allows us to use color as a powerful tool for self-expression, connection, and transformation.

Universal Meanings of Color

Certain colors evoke consistent emotional and psychological responses across cultures and contexts. These universal meanings often stem from nature and shared human experiences.

Red: The Color of Life and Passion

- **Universal Associations**: Red is universally tied to powerful emotions such as love, passion, and anger. It is the color of blood and fire, signifying life, energy, and danger.
- **Applications**:
    - **Alertness**: Red is used in warning signs and stop signals due to its ability to capture attention quickly.
    - **Romance**: Often associated with love and desire, red is a staple in Valentine's Day imagery and romantic branding.

Blue: The Color of Calm and Introspection

- **Universal Associations**: As the color of the sky and water, blue symbolizes tranquility, trust, and stability. It is often associated with introspection and the infinite.
- **Applications**:
    - **Healing**: Used in therapy and meditation spaces to create a sense of calm.
    - **Corporate Trust**: Widely used by financial institutions and tech companies to evoke reliability and professionalism.

Green: The Color of Growth and Renewal

- **Universal Associations**: Green reflects the natural world, symbolizing life, growth, and renewal. It is also tied to balance and health.
- **Applications**:
    - **Eco-Friendliness**: Commonly used in sustainability and environmental branding.
    - **Healing Spaces**: Found in hospitals and wellness centers to promote a sense of peace and rejuvenation.

Yellow: The Color of Joy and Energy

- **Universal Associations**: Yellow is linked to sunlight, warmth, and happiness. It is the color of optimism and energy, but it can also signal caution.
- **Applications**:
    - **Attention-Grabbing**: Used in advertisements and warning signs for its eye-catching nature.
    - **Creative Spaces**: Inspires creativity and positivity in workspaces.

Black: The Color of Power and Mystery

- **Universal Associations**: Black is associated with strength, authority, and elegance. It also signifies mystery, death, and the unknown.
- **Applications**:
    - **Sophistication**: A staple in fashion and luxury branding.
    - **Symbol of Mourning**: Used in funerary traditions worldwide.

White: The Color of Purity and Simplicity

- **Universal Associations**: White symbolizes purity, cleanliness, and new beginnings. It is often associated with peace and clarity.
- **Applications**:
    - **Minimalist Design**: Emphasizes simplicity and cleanliness.
    - **Spiritual Practices**: Used in rituals and ceremonies to symbolize purity and renewal.

The Personal Meanings of Color

While universal associations provide a broad understanding of color meanings, personal experiences and memories add a deeply individual dimension. The colors we love—or avoid—are often shaped by our unique histories.

Memory and Emotion

- **Positive Associations**: A person who has fond childhood memories of playing in a green field may find green comforting and nostalgic.
- **Negative Associations**: Someone who associates red with a traumatic event may feel uneasy or agitated in its presence.

Cultural and Familial Influences

Family traditions and cultural heritage can shape how we perceive and use color. For instance:

- A family that celebrates festivals with vibrant yellows and reds may view these colors as joyful and festive.
- A culture that associates white with mourning may evoke sadness or reflection in its presence.

Mood and Context

Our emotional state and the context in which we encounter a color can also affect its meaning:

- **Mood-Dependent Perception**: A bright yellow room may feel cheerful to a happy person but overwhelming to someone feeling anxious.
- **Contextual Variation**: Red in a romantic setting may signify love, but in a competitive setting, it could symbolize aggression.

The Intersection of Universal and Personal Meanings

The meanings we attribute to colors are rarely static. Universal associations often form the foundation, but personal experiences add layers of complexity. For example:

- Blue's universal association with calmness may be heightened for someone who grew up near the ocean and associates the color with peaceful waves.
- Conversely, someone who experienced a stressful event involving water may find blue unsettling, despite its universal calming connotation.

The Role of Color in Self-Expression

Colors are a powerful medium for expressing identity, mood, and values. From clothing to home decor, the colors we choose say a lot about who we are:

- **Clothing**: Wearing red may signal confidence or a desire to stand out, while wearing black can convey sophistication or a preference for subtlety.
- **Home Decor**: A green living room may reflect a love of nature and a desire for balance, while a predominantly white space may suggest a preference for simplicity and clarity.

Understanding the language of color helps us make intentional choices that align with our emotions and goals.

Practical Applications of Color Language
In Personal Development

- **Mood Management**: Use color intentionally to influence your mood. Surround yourself with calming blues when stressed or energizing yellows when you need a boost.
- **Empowerment**: Choose clothing or accessories in colors that make you feel confident, such as bold reds or powerful blacks.

In Relationships

- **Communication**: Be mindful of how colors affect those around you. For example, decorating a shared space with soft greens and neutrals can create a sense of harmony.
- **Gift Giving**: Consider the recipient's color preferences and the emotional associations of colors when selecting gifts.

In Creativity and Design

- **Art and Design**: Use color strategically to convey messages and evoke specific emotions in your audience.
- **Branding**: Align your brand's color palette with the emotions and values you want to communicate to your target audience.

The Dynamic Nature of Color Meanings

The meanings of color are not fixed; they can evolve over time and adapt to new contexts. Advances in science, cultural shifts, and individual growth continually reshape how we perceive and use color.

For example:

- Green has gained a modern association with sustainability and environmentalism, reflecting the growing global emphasis on eco-consciousness.
- Pink, once considered exclusively feminine in many Western cultures, has become a symbol of empowerment and inclusivity across genders.

Conclusion: Unlocking the Language of Color

The language of color is a dynamic and multifaceted system that bridges the universal and the personal. By understanding both the broad emotional effects of colors and their unique personal meanings, we can use color to enrich our lives, connect with others, and express our true selves.

Part 2: Individual Colors and Their Emotional Codes

Chapter 6: Red: Passion, Energy, and Warning

Red is one of the most evocative and powerful colors in the spectrum, symbolizing a broad range of emotions and ideas. From passion and love to anger and danger, red commands attention and provokes action. Its psychological, cultural, and historical significance make it a color of immense depth and complexity. In this chapter, we explore the meaning of red, its effects on the mind and body, and its role in history, culture, and practical applications.

The Psychology of Red: How It Affects the Mind and Body

Red has a unique ability to influence our emotions and physiological state, making it one of the most stimulating colors in the spectrum.

Emotional Effects

- **Passion and Love**: Red is often associated with strong emotions like love, desire, and passion. Its intensity reflects the depth of human connection and attraction.
- **Anger and Aggression**: Red can also evoke feelings of anger, frustration, or aggression, symbolizing heightened emotional states.
- **Urgency and Excitement**: Red's ability to attract attention makes it a symbol of urgency and excitement, often used in contexts that demand immediate action.

Physiological Effects

- **Increased Heart Rate**: Studies have shown that exposure to red can increase heart rate and blood pressure, signaling the body to prepare for action.
- **Stimulated Appetite**: Red is known to stimulate appetite, which is why it is often used in restaurant branding and food advertisements.
- **Enhanced Performance**: In some contexts, red has been found to boost physical performance, likely due to its stimulating effects on the body.

The Symbolism of Red Across Cultures

The meanings of red vary across cultures, but its intensity and power are universally recognized.

Western Cultures

- **Love and Romance**: In the West, red is synonymous with Valentine's Day, symbolizing love, passion, and intimacy.
- **Warning and Danger**: Red is used in stop signs, warning labels, and emergency signals to convey danger or caution.
- **Power and Prestige**: Red carpets at events symbolize luxury and high status.

Eastern Cultures

- **Good Fortune and Prosperity**: In China, red is a symbol of good luck, joy, and celebration. It is a dominant color during Chinese New Year and weddings.
- **Life and Vitality**: In India, red represents purity, fertility, and power, often worn by brides on their wedding day.

Indigenous and Ancient Cultures

- **Life and Death**: Many indigenous cultures associate red with both life and death, reflecting its ties to blood.
- **Spiritual Power**: In some African cultures, red represents spiritual strength and ancestral power.

Red in Nature: A Color of Survival and Signal

In the natural world, red serves as a powerful visual signal for survival and communication:

- **Attraction**: Many flowers and fruits are red to attract pollinators or signal ripeness.
- **Warning**: Animals like poison dart frogs and red coral snakes use red to warn predators of their toxicity.
- **Energy**: Red sunsets and volcanic eruptions demonstrate the raw energy of nature, adding to the color's association with power and intensity.

The History of Red: A Color of Prestige and Revolution
Throughout history, red has held significant cultural and political meanings:

- **Ancient Civilizations**: In Ancient Egypt, red was associated with the desert and chaos but also used in protective amulets.
- **Medieval Europe**: Red was the color of the Catholic Church and royalty, symbolizing power, sacrifice, and divine authority.
- **Revolutions**: Red has been a symbol of rebellion and revolution, from the French Revolution to modern socialist and communist movements.

The Use of Red in Art and Fashion
Art
Red has been a favorite color of artists for centuries, used to convey emotion, drama, and focus:

- **Renaissance and Baroque Art**: Red was used to highlight religious themes, often symbolizing the blood of Christ or divine love.
- **Modern Art**: Artists like Mark Rothko and Henri Matisse used red to evoke emotion and intensity.

Fashion
Red is a bold and confident color in fashion, often associated with power and attraction:

- **Statement Pieces**: Red dresses or suits are designed to capture attention and exude confidence.
- **Cultural Significance**: In many cultures, red clothing is worn during celebrations to bring good fortune or ward off evil.

Red in Marketing and Branding

Red is one of the most popular colors in marketing due to its ability to evoke strong emotions and drive action:

- **Attention-Grabbing**: Red is used in sale signs and advertisements to create a sense of urgency.
- **Appetite-Stimulation**: Brands like Coca-Cola and McDonald's use red to stimulate appetite and excitement.
- **Emotional Appeal**: Red creates an emotional connection, making it ideal for brands focusing on passion, energy, or love.

The Role of Red in Everyday Life

Red plays a significant role in how we experience the world around us:

- **Interior Design**: Red is often used sparingly in home decor to add warmth and vibrancy, though too much red can feel overwhelming.
- **Sports and Competition**: Red is associated with winning and competitiveness, with studies suggesting that teams wearing red uniforms may have an edge in competitions.
- **Wellness and Therapy**: Red is used in color therapy to stimulate energy and motivation but should be balanced with cooler tones to prevent overstimulation.

Practical Applications of Red

Understanding the psychological and symbolic power of red can help us use it effectively in various aspects of life.

Personal Expression

- **Clothing**: Wearing red can boost confidence, make a bold statement, or attract attention in social or professional settings.
- **Accessories**: A touch of red in accessories can add energy and sophistication to an outfit.

Home and Work Spaces

- **Accent Walls**: A red accent wall can create warmth and energy but should be balanced with neutral tones to avoid overstimulation.
- **Creative Spaces**: Red can stimulate creativity and energy in spaces designed for brainstorming or artistic work.

Health and Fitness

- **Motivation**: Red workout gear or equipment can help boost energy and focus during exercise.
- **Dietary Choices**: Incorporating red foods like tomatoes, strawberries, and peppers into meals can signal vitality and health.

Balancing Red with Other Colors

While red is powerful, it can be overwhelming if overused. Pairing red with complementary colors can balance its intensity:

- **Red and Green**: A classic complementary pairing that creates harmony and contrast.
- **Red and White**: Red paired with white softens its intensity and creates a sense of freshness.
- **Red and Blue**: Balancing the energy of red with the calmness of blue creates a dynamic but stable combination.

Conclusion: The Dual Nature of Red

Red is a color of extremes—passion and danger, love and anger, energy and caution. Its ability to evoke such a wide range of emotions makes it one of the most versatile and impactful colors in the spectrum. By understanding the psychology and symbolism of red, we can harness its power to inspire action, communicate emotion, and enrich our lives.

Chapter 7: Orange: Creativity, Warmth, and Optimism

Orange is a vibrant and dynamic color, exuding energy, enthusiasm, and positivity. As a blend of red's passion and yellow's cheerfulness, orange carries a unique ability to stimulate creativity, foster warmth, and inspire optimism. This chapter dives into the psychological, cultural, and historical significance of orange, explores its role in art and design, and highlights practical ways to incorporate its energy into daily life.

The Psychology of Orange: Energizing and Uplifting

Orange is one of the most stimulating colors, evoking strong emotions and fostering an atmosphere of excitement and positivity.

Emotional Effects

- **Creativity**: Orange stimulates mental activity and creativity, making it an excellent choice for brainstorming and artistic environments.
- **Warmth**: Like a sunset or a roaring fire, orange creates feelings of comfort, warmth, and security.
- **Optimism**: The brightness of orange naturally uplifts moods, making it a color of hope and positivity.

Physiological Effects

- **Energy Boost**: Orange can increase energy levels and physical stamina, encouraging activity and engagement.
- **Appetite Stimulation**: Like red, orange stimulates appetite, which is why it is commonly used in restaurants and food branding.
- **Focus Enhancement**: Its vibrant tones draw attention without the aggressive urgency of red, making it ideal for fostering focus in creative tasks.

The Symbolism of Orange Across Cultures

Orange holds varied meanings across different cultures, often reflecting its dual nature as a warm and energetic color.

Western Cultures

- **Creativity and Enthusiasm**: In the West, orange is often associated with creativity, fun, and adventure.
- **Seasonal Connection**: Orange is tied to autumn and Halloween due to the color of pumpkins and fall leaves.
- **Caution**: Used in safety gear and traffic signs, orange signals caution and visibility.

Eastern Cultures

- **Spirituality**: In Hinduism and Buddhism, saffron orange is a sacred color symbolizing renunciation, purity, and enlightenment.
- **Vitality and Good Fortune**: In some Asian cultures, orange represents happiness, energy, and vitality.

Indigenous and Ancient Cultures

- **Connection to Earth**: In Native American traditions, orange often represents the balance between the earth and the spirit.
- **Celebration**: Orange has been used in traditional ceremonies and festivals to evoke joy and festivity.

Orange in Nature: A Color of Life and Energy

Nature provides abundant examples of orange, reinforcing its association with vitality, energy, and life:

- **Sunsets and Sunrises**: The fiery orange of dawn and dusk signifies transition, renewal, and inspiration.
- **Citrus Fruits**: Oranges, tangerines, and other citrus fruits symbolize health, abundance, and zest for life.
- **Flowers and Wildlife**: Orange flowers like marigolds and animals like tigers embody beauty, power, and vibrancy.

Historical Perspectives on Orange

Orange has held different meanings throughout history, evolving with cultural and societal changes:

- **Ancient Egypt**: Orange pigments made from natural minerals were used in art to represent vitality and endurance.
- **Medieval Europe**: Orange was less prominent due to the rarity of orange dyes but appeared in religious art, symbolizing illumination and enlightenment.
- **Renaissance**: With the advent of new pigments, orange became a symbol of wealth, luxury, and creativity in art.

Orange in Art and Fashion

Art

Artists have long used orange to evoke energy, warmth, and movement:

- **Impressionism**: Painters like Claude Monet used orange to capture the glow of sunlight in landscapes.
- **Modern Art**: Abstract artists like Mark Rothko used orange to evoke emotional intensity and depth.

Fashion

Orange makes a bold statement in fashion, often symbolizing confidence and individuality:

- **Energetic Appeal**: Bright orange garments exude enthusiasm and attract attention.
- **Seasonal Trends**: Earthy orange tones are popular in fall collections, reflecting the warmth of autumn.

Orange in Marketing and Branding

Orange is a versatile color in marketing, often used to appeal to younger, adventurous audiences:

- **Creativity and Playfulness**: Brands like Fanta and Nickelodeon use orange to convey fun and energy.
- **Call to Action**: Orange is effective in buttons and advertisements, encouraging engagement without the urgency of red.
- **Health and Vitality**: Orange is used by wellness brands to evoke energy, health, and happiness.

Practical Applications of Orange

Orange is a dynamic color that can be incorporated into various aspects of life to enhance energy, creativity, and warmth.

Personal Expression

- **Clothing**: Wearing orange communicates confidence, enthusiasm, and a zest for life.
- **Accessories**: Orange scarves, bags, or ties add a pop of energy to neutral outfits.

Home and Work Spaces

- **Creative Spaces**: Incorporate orange in art studios or offices to stimulate ideas and innovation.
- **Living Areas**: Use warm orange tones in living rooms to create a welcoming and cozy atmosphere.
- **Kitchen and Dining**: Orange accents in dining areas can stimulate appetite and conversation.

Events and Celebrations

- **Festivals**: Orange is a vibrant choice for decorations and themes in joyful celebrations.
- **Seasonal Decor**: Use orange to evoke the warmth and nostalgia of autumn or the playfulness of Halloween.

Balancing Orange with Other Colors

To make the most of orange, pair it thoughtfully with complementary or neutral colors:

- **Orange and Blue**: A classic complementary pairing that balances warmth and coolness.
- **Orange and White**: Creates a fresh and modern look that highlights orange's vibrancy.
- **Orange and Earth Tones**: Combining orange with browns and greens evokes the warmth and harmony of nature.

Orange in Wellness and Therapy
Orange is used in wellness and color therapy to energize and uplift:

- **Mood Enhancement**: Orange can help combat feelings of lethargy or sadness by fostering a sense of enthusiasm.
- **Social Connection**: Its warm and inviting nature makes orange an excellent choice for spaces where people gather.
- **Physical Vitality**: Orange is believed to stimulate energy flow in the body, promoting vitality and endurance.

The Dynamic Nature of Orange
Orange is a color of dualities—warmth and energy, creativity and caution. Its dynamic nature allows it to adapt to various contexts and purposes, making it one of the most versatile colors in the spectrum.

Conclusion: Harnessing the Power of Orange
Orange is a color that radiates positivity, creativity, and warmth. By understanding its psychological and symbolic power, we can use orange to inspire innovation, foster connections, and create vibrant, welcoming environments. Whether through art, fashion, or design, orange offers a unique opportunity to energize and uplift our lives.

Chapter 8: Yellow: Happiness, Clarity, and Caution

Yellow is the color of sunshine, optimism, and clarity. It radiates positivity and inspires mental clarity, but it also carries associations with caution and alertness. This dual nature makes yellow one of the most psychologically stimulating colors. In this chapter, we explore the emotional, cultural, and historical significance of yellow, its effects on the human mind and body, and its applications in art, design, and everyday life.

The Psychology of Yellow: A Color of Contrasts

Yellow's psychological effects are as vibrant and multifaceted as the color itself, ranging from uplifting joy to attention-commanding caution.

Emotional Effects

- **Happiness and Positivity**: Yellow is strongly associated with feelings of joy, energy, and optimism. It's the color of sunny days and cheerful dispositions.
- **Mental Clarity**: Yellow stimulates mental activity and intellectual energy, promoting focus and problem-solving.
- **Anxiety and Frustration**: In excessive amounts, yellow can evoke feelings of agitation, frustration, or overstimulation.

Physiological Effects

- **Boosted Energy**: Yellow's brightness can stimulate the nervous system, increasing energy and alertness.
- **Eye Fatigue**: Overexposure to bright yellow can cause eye strain, as the color is highly reflective and stimulating.
- **Appetite Stimulation**: Like red and orange, yellow can increase appetite, making it popular in food branding.

The Symbolism of Yellow Across Cultures

Yellow holds a variety of meanings across cultures, often shaped by its associations with light, gold, and the natural world.

Western Cultures

- **Happiness and Cheerfulness**: In Western cultures, yellow is widely seen as a symbol of joy and positivity.
- **Caution and Warning**: Yellow is used in traffic signs and warning labels to signal caution and demand attention.
- **Ambiguity**: In some contexts, yellow can represent cowardice or deceit, such as in the term "yellow-bellied."

Eastern Cultures

- **Royalty and Spirituality**: In China, yellow is historically associated with emperors and the divine, symbolizing power, wisdom, and prosperity.
- **Sacredness**: In Hinduism and Buddhism, yellow represents learning, knowledge, and spiritual enlightenment.

African and Indigenous Cultures

- **Wealth and Fertility**: In many African cultures, yellow represents wealth, fertility, and the power of the sun.
- **Connection to Nature**: Yellow is often linked to natural elements like flowers, crops, and the cycle of life.

Yellow in Nature: Light, Warmth, and Growth

Yellow is abundant in nature, reinforcing its associations with life, warmth, and vitality:

- **Sunlight**: The golden hues of the sun symbolize energy, growth, and the passage of time.
- **Flowers and Plants**: Yellow flowers like sunflowers, daisies, and marigolds evoke joy and renewal.
- **Animals**: Yellow often serves as a warning color in nature, signaling toxicity or danger, such as in bees and poisonous frogs.

The History of Yellow: From Gold to Modernity

Yellow's history is intertwined with its association with wealth, light, and caution:

- **Ancient Civilizations**: Yellow pigments were derived from natural minerals like ochre and were used in cave paintings and early art to represent the sun and gold.
- **Medieval Europe**: Yellow was associated with both wealth and betrayal. It was used to depict Judas Iscariot in Christian art, symbolizing deceit.
- **The Renaissance**: Artists like Vincent van Gogh used yellow to symbolize emotional intensity, as seen in works like *Sunflowers*.

Yellow in Art and Fashion

Art

Yellow has been a favorite color of artists for its ability to convey light, warmth, and emotion:

- **Impressionism**: Artists like Claude Monet used yellow to capture the glow of sunlight in landscapes.
- **Post-Impressionism**: Vincent van Gogh used intense yellows to convey emotional energy and vitality, as seen in *The Starry Night* and *The Yellow House*.

Fashion

Yellow in fashion is bold and playful, often making a statement:

- **Energy and Joy**: Bright yellow garments exude confidence and positivity.
- **Seasonal Appeal**: Soft yellow tones are popular in spring and summer collections, reflecting renewal and freshness.

Yellow in Marketing and Branding

Yellow is a favorite in marketing due to its ability to grab attention and evoke happiness:

- **Cheerfulness**: Brands like McDonald's and Snapchat use yellow to convey friendliness and energy.
- **Affordability**: Yellow is often used in discount store branding to suggest value and accessibility.
- **Urgency**: Yellow is commonly combined with black in signage to signal caution or action.

The Role of Yellow in Everyday Life

Yellow can have a profound impact on how we perceive and interact with our environment:

- **Interior Design**: Yellow walls can brighten a space and evoke warmth, but too much yellow can feel overwhelming.
- **Workspace Productivity**: Yellow is often used in creative spaces to stimulate ideas and focus.
- **Safety and Visibility**: High-visibility clothing and caution signs use yellow to ensure they are easily noticed.

Practical Applications of Yellow
Personal Expression

- **Clothing**: Wearing yellow can make a bold, cheerful statement, conveying confidence and positivity.
- **Accessories**: A yellow scarf, bag, or jewelry piece can add a pop of energy to an outfit.

Home Decor

- **Accent Walls**: A yellow accent wall can bring light and warmth to a room.
- **Kitchen and Dining**: Yellow in kitchens can create a welcoming and cheerful atmosphere.

Events and Celebrations

- **Festive Themes**: Yellow is an excellent choice for celebrations like birthdays, reflecting joy and liveliness.
- **Seasonal Decor**: Yellow is popular in spring and summer decor, symbolizing growth and renewal.

Balancing Yellow with Other Colors

To make yellow more versatile, it is often paired with other colors to balance its brightness:

- **Yellow and Gray**: A sophisticated combination that tempers yellow's intensity with gray's neutrality.
- **Yellow and Blue**: A complementary pairing that balances warmth and coolness.
- **Yellow and White**: A clean, fresh combination that enhances yellow's brightness.

Yellow in Wellness and Therapy

Yellow is used in wellness practices and color therapy to promote positivity and mental clarity:

- **Mood Enhancement**: Yellow is believed to uplift mood and combat feelings of lethargy or sadness.
- **Mental Stimulation**: It can help improve focus and clarity, making it ideal for workspaces or study areas.
- **Social Connection**: Yellow's warmth fosters feelings of friendliness and openness in social settings.

The Dual Nature of Yellow

Yellow's duality—its ability to evoke happiness and caution—makes it a color of contrasts. While it is associated with joy and light, its overuse or intensity can signal danger or cause overstimulation. This dual nature makes yellow a versatile and complex color, capable of conveying a wide range of emotions and messages.

Conclusion: Embracing the Brightness of Yellow

Yellow is the color of joy, clarity, and energy, bringing light and warmth wherever it is used. By understanding its psychological and symbolic power, we can use yellow to inspire creativity, enhance spaces, and communicate effectively. Whether through design, fashion, or daily life, yellow offers a vibrant tool to uplift and energize.

Chapter 9: Green: Growth, Balance, and Renewal

Green is the color of life, renewal, and harmony. It is deeply intertwined with nature, symbolizing growth, balance, and vitality. Beyond its physical associations, green exerts a powerful influence on our emotions and well-being, offering a sense of calm and equilibrium. In this chapter, we delve into the psychological, cultural, and historical significance of green, its applications in art and design, and practical ways to incorporate its restorative energy into daily life.

The Psychology of Green: A Color of Harmony

Green has a unique psychological effect, combining the energizing properties of yellow with the calming qualities of blue. Its versatility makes it a symbol of balance and tranquility.

Emotional Effects

- **Growth and Renewal**: Green symbolizes new beginnings, reflecting its association with spring, plants, and life cycles.
- **Calmness and Relaxation**: Green promotes a sense of calm, reducing stress and fostering mental clarity.
- **Envy and Jealousy**: While predominantly positive, green also has a historical association with envy and jealousy, as in the phrase "green with envy."

Physiological Effects

- **Stress Reduction**: Exposure to green has been shown to lower heart rates and cortisol levels, promoting relaxation.
- **Improved Focus**: Green environments, such as natural landscapes, enhance concentration and cognitive performance.
- **Healing and Restoration**: Green is often used in hospitals and wellness centers to create a soothing atmosphere.

The Symbolism of Green Across Cultures

Green holds varied meanings across cultures, reflecting its universal ties to nature and life, as well as its cultural interpretations.

Western Cultures

- **Nature and Sustainability**: Green is the universal symbol of environmentalism, representing eco-consciousness and sustainability.
- **Luck and Prosperity**: In Western traditions, green is associated with good fortune, particularly in symbols like four-leaf clovers and leprechauns.
- **Jealousy and Ambition**: Historically, green has also been linked to jealousy and greed, as seen in Shakespeare's reference to "the green-eyed monster."

Eastern Cultures

- **Health and Fertility**: In many Asian cultures, green symbolizes health, vitality, and fertility.
- **Youth and Harmony**: Green is associated with youth, peace, and renewal, aligning with its natural connotations.

African and Indigenous Cultures

- **Life and Abundance**: Green often represents the land, fertility, and prosperity in African cultures.
- **Spiritual Growth**: In many indigenous cultures, green signifies spiritual and emotional growth, tying humans to the natural world.

Green in Nature: The Color of Life

Green dominates the natural world, symbolizing life, growth, and vitality:

- **Plants and Trees**: Chlorophyll, the pigment responsible for green in plants, is vital for photosynthesis, making green the color of life itself.
- **Spring and Renewal**: Green is synonymous with spring, representing renewal and the cycle of life.
- **Balance and Ecosystems**: In nature, green reflects balance and harmony, as seen in lush forests and thriving ecosystems.

The History of Green: From Sacred Symbol to Modern Icon
Green's historical significance spans sacred meanings, practical uses, and evolving cultural interpretations:

- **Ancient Civilizations**: In Ancient Egypt, green was associated with fertility and rebirth, symbolized by Osiris, the god of the afterlife and vegetation.
- **Medieval Europe**: Green represented love and fertility but was also linked to the unpredictable forces of nature and fairy folk in folklore.
- **The Renaissance and Beyond**: Green gained prominence in art and fashion, symbolizing wealth and refinement, especially with the advent of more stable green pigments.

Green in Art and Fashion
Art
Green has played a vital role in art, symbolizing nature, emotion, and balance:

- **Renaissance Art**: Artists used green to depict lush landscapes and symbolize fertility and renewal.
- **Romanticism**: Green became a symbol of the sublime in nature, representing untamed beauty and emotional depth.
- **Modern Art**: Contemporary artists use green to explore themes of ecology, sustainability, and the relationship between humans and nature.

Fashion
Green in fashion communicates balance, freshness, and individuality:

- **Earthy and Natural**: Olive and sage greens are popular for their connection to nature and timeless appeal.
- **Bold Statements**: Emerald green and bright shades make strong, confident statements.
- **Eco-Friendly Trends**: Green is often used to signify sustainable and ethical fashion choices.

Green in Marketing and Branding
Green is a versatile color in branding, often used to convey trust, health, and eco-consciousness:

- **Eco-Conscious Brands**: Companies focused on sustainability and environmentalism frequently use green to symbolize their mission.
- **Health and Wellness**: Green is popular in health food brands and wellness products, representing vitality and freshness.

- **Finance and Growth**: Green is used in financial branding to symbolize wealth, stability, and growth.

The Role of Green in Everyday Life

Green is a color that seamlessly integrates into daily life, enhancing spaces, moods, and experiences:

- **Interior Design**: Green walls or accents bring a sense of nature and tranquility indoors, making spaces feel more inviting.
- **Outdoor Spaces**: Incorporating green plants into living and workspaces improves air quality and mental well-being.
- **Clothing and Accessories**: Wearing green conveys balance, confidence, and a connection to nature.

Practical Applications of Green
Personal Expression

- **Clothing**: Green outfits reflect confidence, renewal, and an appreciation for nature.
- **Jewelry and Accessories**: Emeralds and other green gemstones symbolize wealth and vitality.

Home and Work Spaces

- **Living Rooms**: Soft green tones create a calming and welcoming atmosphere.
- **Workspaces**: Green promotes focus and productivity, making it ideal for offices.
- **Gardens and Balconies**: Adding plants and greenery to outdoor spaces fosters relaxation and a sense of connection to nature.

Events and Celebrations

- **Weddings and Celebrations**: Green is often used in decor to symbolize new beginnings and growth.
- **Seasonal Decor**: Green is central to spring and Christmas themes, representing life and renewal.

Balancing Green with Other Colors

Green pairs beautifully with other colors, enhancing its versatility:

- **Green and White**: Creates a fresh, clean, and peaceful aesthetic.
- **Green and Gold**: Adds a touch of luxury and sophistication.
- **Green and Brown**: Evokes earthy, natural themes, emphasizing harmony and grounding.

Green in Wellness and Therapy

Green is a key color in wellness practices and color therapy, promoting healing and balance:

- **Stress Relief**: Green environments reduce stress and foster a sense of calm.
- **Physical Healing**: Green is believed to stimulate healing and recovery, aligning with its natural associations.
- **Emotional Balance**: Green helps stabilize emotions, promoting a sense of harmony and well-being.

The Timeless Power of Green

Green's connection to life, nature, and balance makes it a timeless and universal symbol. Its versatility allows it to adapt to various contexts, from calming interiors to bold fashion statements, and its psychological effects make it an essential color for promoting health and harmony.

Conclusion: Harnessing the Energy of Green

Green is a color that embodies renewal, growth, and balance, making it an essential part of our visual and emotional language. By understanding its psychological and symbolic significance, we can use green to enhance our environments, inspire creativity, and promote well-being. Whether through fashion, design, or personal expression, green offers a pathway to harmony and vitality.

Chapter 10: Blue: Calm, Trust, and Introspection

Blue is one of the most universally beloved colors, associated with calmness, trust, and introspection. Its prevalence in nature—in the vast skies and tranquil waters—makes it a color that soothes the mind and fosters deep thought. From its psychological effects to its cultural significance and practical applications, blue is a powerful and multifaceted color. This chapter explores blue's emotional resonance, historical importance, and role in art, fashion, and daily life.

The Psychology of Blue: Serenity and Stability

Blue has a profound psychological impact, often evoking feelings of calm, trust, and contemplation. Its effects are rooted in both nature and biology.

Emotional Effects

- **Calmness and Relaxation**: Blue is known for its ability to reduce stress and promote tranquility, making it a popular choice for environments where relaxation is desired.
- **Trust and Dependability**: Blue conveys reliability and stability, which is why it is often used in professional and corporate settings.
- **Introspection and Depth**: Blue encourages self-reflection and introspection, fostering creativity and problem-solving.

Physiological Effects

- **Lowered Heart Rate**: Exposure to blue has been shown to lower heart rates and blood pressure, contributing to a sense of physical calmness.
- **Cooling Effect**: Blue is associated with cooler temperatures, creating a refreshing and soothing atmosphere.
- **Improved Focus**: Blue promotes mental clarity and focus, making it ideal for workspaces and study areas.

The Symbolism of Blue Across Cultures

Blue carries deep and varied meanings in different cultures, often reflecting its natural associations with the sky, water, and the infinite.

Western Cultures

- **Trust and Authority**: In Western societies, blue is associated with professionalism and authority, often used in uniforms and corporate branding.
- **Peace and Sadness**: Blue represents peace and calm but also has ties to melancholy, as seen in the term "feeling blue."
- **Faith and Divinity**: Blue is often linked to religious imagery, symbolizing purity and divine connection.

Eastern Cultures

- **Spirituality and Protection**: In many Eastern cultures, blue is considered a protective and spiritual color. For instance, in Hinduism, blue is associated with Krishna, symbolizing divine love and compassion.
- **Immortality and Wisdom**: In Chinese culture, blue symbolizes immortality and wisdom, often connected to the heavens.

Indigenous and African Cultures

- **Connection to the Spirit World**: Many indigenous cultures associate blue with the spirit world and healing.
- **Sacredness**: In African traditions, blue is often linked to sacred rituals and protection.

Blue in Nature: Vastness and Serenity

Nature provides abundant examples of blue, reinforcing its associations with peace, infinity, and purity:

- **Skies and Oceans**: Blue dominates the natural world, symbolizing vastness, freedom, and tranquility.
- **Ice and Snow**: The bluish hues of glaciers and ice reflect the cooling, calming properties of the color.
- **Flowers and Wildlife**: Blue flowers like forget-me-nots and bluebells, as well as birds like the blue jay, evoke a sense of delicate beauty and uniqueness.

The History of Blue: From Rarity to Reverence

Blue's history is as rich as the color itself, transitioning from a rare pigment to one of the most celebrated colors:

- **Ancient Civilizations**: In Ancient Egypt, blue was associated with the gods and the heavens. Lapis lazuli, a rare and valuable stone, was used in jewelry and sacred art.
- **Medieval Europe**: During the Middle Ages, blue gained prominence in religious art, symbolizing the Virgin Mary's purity and divine grace.
- **The Renaissance and Beyond**: Advances in pigment production, such as the creation of ultramarine and cobalt blue, made blue a favored color in Renaissance art.

Blue in Art and Fashion

Art

Blue has been a cornerstone of artistic expression for centuries, symbolizing emotion, depth, and serenity:

- **Renaissance Art**: Artists like Leonardo da Vinci and Michelangelo used blue to depict divinity and heavenly realms.
- **Modern Art**: Pablo Picasso's "Blue Period" exemplifies blue's ability to convey melancholy and introspection.

Fashion

Blue is a timeless and versatile color in fashion, reflecting sophistication and calm:

- **Professionalism**: Navy blue is a staple in business attire, conveying authority and trust.
- **Casual Comfort**: Denim, a universally popular fabric, highlights blue's relaxed and approachable qualities.
- **Luxury and Elegance**: Deep shades like royal blue and sapphire convey sophistication and luxury.

Blue in Marketing and Branding

Blue is one of the most frequently used colors in branding due to its universal appeal and psychological effects:

- **Trust and Reliability**: Financial institutions and tech companies, such as Facebook, Twitter, and IBM, use blue to communicate trustworthiness and professionalism.
- **Calm and Reassurance**: Blue is often used in healthcare branding to create a sense of safety and care.

- **Versatility**: Blue's broad appeal makes it a popular choice across industries, from travel to education.

The Role of Blue in Everyday Life

Blue enhances daily life by fostering calmness, focus, and a sense of connection to the larger world:

- **Interior Design**: Blue walls or decor bring a sense of peace and spaciousness to a room.
- **Workspaces**: Light blue tones promote focus and productivity in offices or study areas.
- **Clothing and Accessories**: Wearing blue communicates reliability, calm, and approachability.

Practical Applications of Blue
Personal Expression

- **Clothing**: Blue suits exude professionalism, while lighter shades are perfect for casual, relaxed settings.
- **Accessories**: Blue gemstones like sapphires and aquamarines add elegance and depth.

Home Decor

- **Bedrooms**: Blue is ideal for bedrooms due to its calming effect, promoting restful sleep.
- **Bathrooms**: Shades of blue in bathrooms evoke cleanliness and freshness.
- **Living Areas**: Incorporating blue in living spaces fosters a tranquil and welcoming atmosphere.

Events and Celebrations

- **Weddings**: Blue is a popular choice for weddings, symbolizing fidelity and devotion.
- **Corporate Events**: Blue is often used in professional gatherings to convey trust and authority.

Balancing Blue with Other Colors

Blue's versatility allows it to pair beautifully with other colors, enhancing its impact:

- **Blue and White**: A classic combination that conveys freshness and purity.
- **Blue and Yellow**: A complementary pairing that balances blue's calmness with yellow's energy.
- **Blue and Gray**: Creates a sophisticated and modern aesthetic, ideal for professional or minimalist spaces.

Blue in Wellness and Therapy

Blue is a cornerstone of wellness and color therapy, promoting mental and emotional balance:

- **Stress Relief**: Blue environments reduce anxiety and create a sense of peace.
- **Healing and Recovery**: Blue is used in medical facilities to foster a sense of calm and stability.
- **Focus and Introspection**: Blue supports deep thought and introspection, making it a valuable color for meditation and creativity.

The Timeless Power of Blue

Blue's enduring appeal lies in its ability to evoke calmness, trust, and introspection. Whether in nature, art, or everyday life, blue connects us to both the vastness of the world and the depths of our own minds.

Conclusion: Embracing the Depth of Blue

Blue is a color that embodies serenity, stability, and profound introspection. By understanding its psychological and symbolic power, we can harness blue to create environments, foster trust, and inspire thoughtful reflection. Whether through design, fashion, or personal expression, blue offers a timeless and universal language of calm and connection.

Chapter 11: Purple: Imagination, Royalty, and Spirituality

Purple is a color steeped in history, symbolism, and emotion. A blend of calming blue and energizing red, purple represents the perfect balance between two contrasting forces. Often associated with imagination, royalty, and spirituality, purple has been revered throughout history for its rarity and richness. In this chapter, we delve into the psychological, cultural, and historical significance of purple, its role in art and design, and its applications in everyday life.

The Psychology of Purple: A Color of Balance and Creativity

Purple is a complex and intriguing color that stimulates the imagination and evokes feelings of luxury and mysticism.

Emotional Effects

- **Creativity and Imagination**: Purple inspires creativity and innovation, making it a favorite among artists, writers, and designers.
- **Mystery and Spirituality**: With its deep and enigmatic hues, purple is often associated with the mystical and the unknown.
- **Luxury and Sophistication**: Purple's historical ties to royalty and wealth continue to evoke feelings of grandeur and exclusivity.

Physiological Effects

- **Mental Stimulation**: Purple encourages deep thinking and introspection, fostering a sense of curiosity and exploration.
- **Relaxation and Balance**: The calming influence of blue in purple tones promotes relaxation, while the energizing qualities of red add vibrancy and focus.
- **Heightened Awareness**: Purple is believed to stimulate the pineal gland, enhancing spiritual awareness and intuition.

The Symbolism of Purple Across Cultures

Purple carries diverse meanings across cultures, often tied to its associations with wealth, power, and spirituality.

Western Cultures

- **Royalty and Nobility**: In Western history, purple has been the color of kings, queens, and emperors due to its rarity and cost.
- **Creativity and Individuality**: Purple represents nonconformity and imagination, often associated with artists and free thinkers.
- **Mourning and Remembrance**: In some Western traditions, darker shades of purple symbolize mourning and introspection.

Eastern Cultures

- **Spirituality and Enlightenment**: In Hinduism and Buddhism, purple is associated with higher consciousness, meditation, and the crown chakra.
- **Mysticism and Sacredness**: In China, purple is linked to the cosmos and divine energy, symbolizing harmony and spiritual power.

Indigenous and African Cultures

- **Healing and Spiritual Connection**: In some indigenous cultures, purple represents healing and a connection to the spiritual realm.
- **Wealth and Status**: In African traditions, purple is often a symbol of affluence, prestige, and power.

Purple in Nature: Rare and Enchanting

Purple is a relatively rare color in nature, adding to its mystique and value:

- **Flowers**: Lilacs, lavender, and violets embody the beauty and delicacy of purple in the natural world.
- **Fruits and Vegetables**: Purple foods like grapes, eggplants, and blueberries symbolize health and abundance.
- **Animals**: Rare animals, such as purple starfish or certain butterfly species, showcase purple's uniqueness in the animal kingdom.

The History of Purple: From Sacred Dye to Modern Icon

Purple's history is rooted in its rarity and association with power and spirituality:

- **Ancient Civilizations**: The Phoenicians were among the first to create Tyrian purple dye, derived from sea snails. This labor-intensive process made purple a symbol of wealth and exclusivity.
- **Medieval Europe**: Purple was reserved for the nobility and clergy, signifying divine authority and social hierarchy.
- **Modern Era**: Advances in synthetic dyes during the 19th century made purple accessible to the masses, yet it retained its luxurious and creative connotations.

Purple in Art and Fashion

Art

Purple has been used throughout art history to evoke emotion, mystery, and luxury:

- **Renaissance and Baroque Art**: Purple was used sparingly in religious paintings to signify divinity and spiritual importance.
- **Modern Art**: Artists like Georgia O'Keeffe and Wassily Kandinsky used purple to explore abstraction and emotional depth.

Fashion

Purple in fashion remains a symbol of elegance, creativity, and individuality:

- **Regal Attire**: Deep purples, like royal and plum, convey sophistication and high status.
- **Bold Statements**: Bright purples and lilac shades are used to make bold, creative fashion choices.
- **Gender Neutrality**: Purple's balance of blue and red makes it a versatile and inclusive color in fashion.

Purple in Marketing and Branding

Purple's unique psychological effects make it a valuable tool in branding and marketing:

- **Luxury and Prestige**: Brands like Cadbury and Hallmark use purple to convey exclusivity and high quality.
- **Creativity and Innovation**: Companies like Yahoo and Twitch use purple to appeal to creative and tech-savvy audiences.
- **Spiritual and Holistic Brands**: Purple is often used in wellness and holistic branding to symbolize balance, healing, and spirituality.

The Role of Purple in Everyday Life

Purple enhances daily life by fostering creativity, introspection, and a sense of luxury:

- **Interior Design**: Purple adds depth and sophistication to interiors, from regal violet accents to calming lavender tones.
- **Workspaces**: Purple can inspire innovation and focus in creative workspaces.
- **Fashion and Accessories**: Wearing purple communicates individuality, confidence, and a connection to imagination.

Practical Applications of Purple
Personal Expression

- **Clothing**: Purple outfits showcase creativity, elegance, and a willingness to stand out.
- **Jewelry and Accessories**: Amethysts and other purple gemstones symbolize spirituality and sophistication.

Home Decor

- **Bedrooms**: Soft purples like lavender create a calming atmosphere, ideal for restful sleep.
- **Living Areas**: Deep purples add a touch of luxury and drama to communal spaces.
- **Creative Spaces**: Purple is perfect for art studios and writing rooms, fostering imagination and focus.

Events and Celebrations

- **Weddings**: Purple symbolizes devotion and romance, making it a popular wedding color.
- **Festivals and Parties**: Bright purples add energy and excitement to celebratory events.

Balancing Purple with Other Colors

Purple pairs beautifully with a variety of colors to create dynamic and harmonious combinations:

- **Purple and Gold**: A classic combination that exudes luxury and grandeur.
- **Purple and Green**: Balances purple's mysticism with green's natural energy.
- **Purple and Gray**: Creates a sophisticated and modern aesthetic.

Purple in Wellness and Therapy

Purple is widely used in wellness and color therapy to promote spiritual growth and emotional balance:

- **Spiritual Healing**: Purple is associated with the crown chakra, representing higher consciousness and spiritual connection.
- **Stress Reduction**: Light purples like lavender have a calming effect, reducing anxiety and promoting relaxation.
- **Creative Energy**: Purple stimulates creativity and introspection, making it a powerful tool for self-discovery and personal growth.

The Dual Nature of Purple

Purple's duality—combining the passion of red with the calm of blue—makes it a color of balance and complexity. It can evoke a wide range of emotions and ideas, from luxury and power to mystery and creativity.

Conclusion: Embracing the Mystique of Purple

Purple is a color that bridges the worlds of imagination, royalty, and spirituality. By understanding its psychological and symbolic significance, we can use purple to inspire creativity, elevate environments, and connect with higher levels of consciousness. Whether through art, fashion, or personal spaces, purple offers a pathway to self-expression, sophistication, and introspection.

Chapter 12: Pink: Compassion, Love, and Gentleness

Pink is a color often associated with tenderness, warmth, and affection. Its blend of passionate red and calming white gives it a unique ability to evoke feelings of compassion, love, and gentleness. While historically seen as a feminine color, pink has evolved to symbolize universal themes of care, nurturing, and emotional healing. In this chapter, we will explore the psychological, cultural, and historical significance of pink, its role in art and design, and its applications in everyday life.

The Psychology of Pink: Emotional Softness and Warmth

Pink is a soothing and uplifting color that appeals to our emotions, encouraging empathy, connection, and a sense of safety.

Emotional Effects

- **Love and Romance**: Pink represents love and affection in its gentlest form, symbolizing unconditional care and nurturing relationships.
- **Compassion and Empathy**: The warmth of pink fosters emotional connection, promoting feelings of understanding and kindness.
- **Playfulness and Joy**: Bright shades of pink are associated with youthful energy, fun, and creativity.

Physiological Effects

- **Calming Effect**: Soft pink tones have a calming influence, reducing aggression and anxiety. This is why pink is sometimes used in environments designed to promote relaxation or resolve conflict.
- **Invigorating Brightness**: Brighter pinks can energize and uplift, sparking creativity and enthusiasm.
- **Sense of Comfort**: The warmth of pink creates a sense of emotional safety, fostering feelings of comfort and security.

The Symbolism of Pink Across Cultures

Pink's meanings vary across cultures, reflecting its connections to love, femininity, and celebration.

Western Cultures

- **Femininity and Softness**: In Western societies, pink has traditionally been associated with femininity, sweetness, and gentleness.
- **Romance**: Pink is a staple in romantic imagery, particularly during Valentine's Day, symbolizing affection and partnership.
- **Youth and Innocence**: Light pinks are often linked to childhood, especially in depictions of young girls and innocence.

Eastern Cultures

- **Celebration and Vitality**: In Japan, pink represents the blooming of cherry blossoms, symbolizing life's fleeting beauty and renewal.
- **Romance and Youth**: Pink is celebrated for its connection to love, vitality, and youthful energy in many Asian cultures.

Global Trends

- **Inclusivity**: In recent years, pink has become a color of inclusion and progress, often used in social movements to promote compassion and equality.
- **Empowerment**: Bright, bold pinks are increasingly used to convey strength and confidence, breaking traditional gender stereotypes.

Pink in Nature: Beauty and Vitality

Pink is abundant in nature, enhancing its association with growth, beauty, and life:

- **Flowers**: Roses, peonies, and cherry blossoms showcase pink's delicate and romantic qualities.
- **Sunrises and Sunsets**: Pink skies evoke a sense of awe and tranquility, symbolizing beginnings and transitions.

- **Animals**: Flamingos and pink river dolphins illustrate the unique and striking beauty of pink in the animal kingdom.

The History of Pink: From Luxury to Inclusivity

Pink's historical journey is a testament to its versatility and evolving significance:

- **18th Century Europe**: Pink was a color of luxury and refinement, worn by men and women in aristocratic circles.
- **20th Century**: By the mid-20th century, pink became associated with femininity due to marketing trends, particularly in baby clothing and consumer products.
- **Modern Era**: Pink has transcended traditional gender roles, becoming a color of empowerment, activism, and universal love.

Pink in Art and Fashion

Art

Pink has been used in art to convey warmth, softness, and emotional depth:

- **Impressionism**: Artists like Claude Monet used pink to depict the beauty of nature, particularly in floral and sunrise scenes.
- **Contemporary Art**: Bold uses of pink in modern art challenge traditional stereotypes, making statements about identity and societal norms.

Fashion

Pink in fashion ranges from subtle elegance to bold statements:

- **Soft Pinks**: Pale shades like blush and rose quartz are associated with sophistication and romance.
- **Bright Pinks**: Vibrant pinks like fuchsia and magenta convey energy, confidence, and individuality.
- **Gender-Neutral Trends**: Pink has become a symbol of gender inclusivity, breaking free from its traditionally feminine associations.

Pink in Marketing and Branding

Pink is widely used in branding to convey warmth, playfulness, and emotional connection:

- **Compassion and Care**: Brands like Breast Cancer Awareness use pink to symbolize care, support, and solidarity.
- **Youthfulness and Fun**: Companies like Barbie and T-Mobile use pink to appeal to playful and energetic audiences.
- **Luxury and Sophistication**: High-end brands incorporate soft pinks to create an elegant and refined aesthetic.

The Role of Pink in Everyday Life
Pink enhances environments and personal expression, adding warmth, comfort, and joy:

- **Interior Design**: Pink walls or decor create cozy and inviting spaces, ideal for bedrooms, nurseries, and living areas.
- **Workspaces**: Light pink tones can foster creativity and reduce stress, making them suitable for home offices or studios.
- **Fashion and Accessories**: Incorporating pink into clothing or accessories adds a touch of vibrancy and personality.

Practical Applications of Pink
Personal Expression

- **Clothing**: Soft pink garments exude romance and gentleness, while bright pinks make bold, confident statements.
- **Jewelry and Accessories**: Pink gemstones like rose quartz and pink sapphires symbolize love and compassion.

Home Decor

- **Living Areas**: Pale pink accents create a warm and calming atmosphere in communal spaces.
- **Bedrooms**: Blush tones are ideal for bedrooms, promoting relaxation and intimacy.
- **Bathrooms**: Bright pinks add energy and playfulness to small spaces.

Events and Celebrations

- **Romantic Occasions**: Pink is a popular choice for weddings, symbolizing love and tenderness.
- **Festive Themes**: Pink is used in celebrations like baby showers and gender reveals for its joyful and welcoming nature.

Balancing Pink with Other Colors
Pink pairs beautifully with a range of colors, enhancing its emotional impact:

- **Pink and White**: A classic combination that conveys purity, softness, and romance.
- **Pink and Gray**: Adds a touch of sophistication, balancing pink's warmth with gray's neutrality.
- **Pink and Green**: Evokes freshness and vitality, reflecting the harmony of nature.

Pink in Wellness and Therapy

Pink plays an important role in wellness and color therapy, fostering emotional healing and compassion:

- **Stress Reduction**: Soft pink tones calm the mind and reduce feelings of anxiety or tension.
- **Emotional Healing**: Pink encourages self-love, acceptance, and empathy, making it valuable in therapeutic settings.
- **Energy and Creativity**: Brighter shades of pink invigorate the mind, inspiring action and innovation.

The Dual Nature of Pink

Pink's duality as both a calming and energizing color makes it unique. While light pinks embody gentleness and tranquility, bold pinks exude vibrancy and strength. This versatility allows pink to resonate with a wide range of emotions and contexts.

Conclusion: Embracing the Tender Power of Pink

Pink is a color that embodies compassion, love, and gentleness while also inspiring energy and creativity. By understanding its psychological and symbolic significance, we can use pink to create nurturing environments, foster emotional connections, and express individuality. Whether through design, fashion, or personal spaces, pink offers a palette of possibilities for warmth, joy, and empowerment.

Chapter 13: White: Purity, Simplicity, and New Beginnings

White is the color of light, purity, and clarity. It represents simplicity and new beginnings, evoking a sense of openness and possibility. In cultures around the world, white carries profound symbolic meanings, from spiritual renewal to minimalism in modern design. As the presence of all colors in light or the absence of color in pigment, white holds a unique place in the spectrum. This chapter explores the psychological, cultural, and historical significance of white, its applications in art and design, and its role in everyday life.

The Psychology of White: Clarity and Calm

White has a profound psychological impact, promoting feelings of cleanliness, peace, and balance. Its neutrality makes it a versatile and universally appealing color.

Emotional Effects

- **Purity and Innocence**: White is often associated with cleanliness, innocence, and new beginnings, symbolizing a blank slate.
- **Calmness and Simplicity**: The simplicity of white creates a serene and uncluttered environment, reducing mental distractions and promoting focus.
- **Coldness and Sterility**: While often calming, excessive use of white can feel impersonal or sterile, especially in clinical settings.

Physiological Effects

- **Visual Rest**: White provides visual rest, allowing the mind to relax and focus.
- **Space Perception**: White creates an illusion of space, making rooms appear larger and more open.
- **Neutrality and Balance**: White balances brighter colors, creating harmony in design and reducing overstimulation.

The Symbolism of White Across Cultures
White carries a rich array of meanings across cultures, often rooted in its associations with light, cleanliness, and spiritual purity.
Western Cultures

- **Purity and Celebration**: In Western societies, white is the color of weddings, symbolizing purity, innocence, and new beginnings.
- **Cleanliness and Minimalism**: White is associated with hygiene and modernity, often seen in minimalist design.
- **Surrender and Peace**: A white flag universally symbolizes truce or surrender.

Eastern Cultures

- **Mourning and Reverence**: In many Eastern cultures, white is the color of mourning and funerals, representing the transition to the afterlife.
- **Spirituality and Enlightenment**: White often symbolizes spiritual awakening and divine presence in religious practices.

Global Trends

- **Neutrality and Modernity**: In global design trends, white is used to create a sense of openness, neutrality, and sophistication.
- **Inclusivity**: As a neutral color, white is often seen as inclusive, providing a base for the addition of other colors.

White in Nature: Light and Space
White is prevalent in nature, symbolizing purity, renewal, and balance:

- **Snow and Ice**: White landscapes evoke a sense of tranquility and transformation during winter.
- **Clouds and Light**: White clouds and bright sunlight symbolize clarity and optimism.
- **Flowers and Animals**: White flowers like lilies and animals like doves represent purity, peace, and beauty.

The History of White: Sacred and Minimalist

White's historical significance is tied to its associations with light, spirituality, and simplicity:

- **Ancient Civilizations**: In Ancient Egypt and Greece, white symbolized sacredness and divine presence, often used in temples and ceremonies.
- **Medieval Europe**: White was associated with the Virgin Mary and the divine, symbolizing purity and holiness in religious art.
- **Modern Minimalism**: In the 20th century, white became the hallmark of minimalist design, representing simplicity and modernity.

White in Art and Fashion

Art

White has been a central element in art, representing light, space, and purity:

- **Classical Art**: White marble was used in sculptures to convey timeless beauty and perfection.
- **Modern Art**: Artists like Kazimir Malevich explored white's abstract and conceptual potential, as seen in *White on White*.

Fashion

White is a timeless color in fashion, symbolizing elegance and sophistication:

- **Weddings**: White wedding dresses symbolize purity and tradition in many cultures.
- **Casual Wear**: White shirts and dresses offer versatility and a sense of freshness.
- **Luxury and Simplicity**: White is used in high-end fashion to convey understated elegance.

White in Marketing and Branding

White is widely used in branding to convey simplicity, purity, and professionalism:

- **Cleanliness and Hygiene**: Brands like Apple and Nike use white to emphasize modernity and innovation.
- **Neutrality and Flexibility**: White backgrounds are common in websites and packaging, providing a clean slate for other design elements.
- **Health and Wellness**: White is often used in healthcare and wellness branding to convey cleanliness and trust.

The Role of White in Everyday Life

White enhances environments and personal expression by creating a sense of balance and openness:

- **Interior Design**: White walls and decor create a fresh, airy atmosphere, ideal for homes and offices.
- **Personal Style**: Wearing white communicates simplicity, elegance, and confidence.
- **Workspaces**: White promotes focus and organization, making it a popular choice for offices.

Practical Applications of White
Personal Expression

- **Clothing**: White garments symbolize sophistication and freshness, suitable for formal and casual occasions.
- **Accessories**: White watches, bags, and jewelry add a touch of elegance to any outfit.

Home Decor

- **Living Spaces**: White walls and furniture create an open, modern aesthetic.
- **Bedrooms**: White bedding and curtains promote relaxation and a sense of cleanliness.
- **Kitchens and Bathrooms**: White tiles and fixtures emphasize hygiene and simplicity.

Events and Celebrations

- **Weddings**: White is the quintessential wedding color, symbolizing new beginnings and commitment.
- **Religious Ceremonies**: White is often used in baptisms, confirmations, and other spiritual events.

Balancing White with Other Colors
White pairs beautifully with other colors, enhancing its versatility:

- **White and Black**: A classic combination that conveys sophistication and balance.
- **White and Blue**: Evokes calmness and freshness, often used in coastal or nautical themes.
- **White and Gold**: Adds a touch of luxury and warmth to white's simplicity.

White in Wellness and Therapy
White plays a significant role in wellness practices, symbolizing clarity and renewal:

- **Mental Clarity**: White spaces encourage focus and a sense of mental organization.
- **Emotional Balance**: White fosters a sense of peace and neutrality, reducing stress and over-thinking.
- **Healing Environments**: White is used in hospitals and wellness centers to promote cleanliness and calm.

The Dual Nature of White
While white symbolizes purity and simplicity, it can also feel stark or impersonal if overused. Balancing white with textures, patterns, or complementary colors prevents it from appearing too sterile.

Conclusion: Embracing the Clarity of White
White is a color of purity, simplicity, and renewal, offering a blank canvas for creativity and expression. By understanding its psychological and symbolic significance, we can use white to create harmonious environments, foster focus, and celebrate new beginnings. Whether in art, fashion, or everyday life, white remains a timeless symbol of possibility and peace.

Chapter 14: Black: Mystery, Power, and Elegance

Black is the color of sophistication, mystery, and authority. As the absence of light and a contrast to all other colors, black holds a unique position in the spectrum. It is a color of dualities: associated with both elegance and fear, beginnings and endings, power and vulnerability. From its use in art and fashion to its role in cultural symbolism and personal expression, black has a profound impact on our perceptions and emotions. This chapter explores the psychological, cultural, and historical significance of black, its applications in design and branding, and how it shapes our everyday lives.

The Psychology of Black: Depth and Authority

Black is a powerful and complex color that evokes a range of psychological and emotional responses, often dependent on context.

Emotional Effects

- **Mystery and Intrigue**: Black is associated with the unknown, creating an air of mystery and curiosity.
- **Power and Authority**: Black conveys strength, confidence, and control, making it a favorite in formal settings and leadership roles.
- **Sadness and Fear**: Black is also linked to mourning, loss, and the subconscious, evoking feelings of introspection or unease.

Physiological Effects

- **Focus and Clarity**: Black's starkness creates a sense of focus and concentration, often used to highlight other colors or elements.
- **Calming or Overwhelming**: While black can feel grounding and secure, too much of it can create a heavy or oppressive atmosphere.
- **Visual Contrast**: Black provides the strongest contrast, making it an essential element in design and visual communication.

The Symbolism of Black Across Cultures

Black carries diverse and sometimes opposing meanings across cultures, reflecting its associations with mystery, power, and the unknown.

Western Cultures

- **Mourning and Death**: In Western societies, black is traditionally worn at funerals, symbolizing grief and respect.
- **Formality and Sophistication**: Black is a staple in formal attire, such as tuxedos and evening gowns, representing elegance and refinement.
- **Rebellion and Individuality**: Black is often associated with countercultures, such as punk and goth movements, symbolizing nonconformity and self-expression.

Eastern Cultures

- **New Beginnings**: In some Eastern traditions, black represents beginnings and the potential for growth.
- **Authority and Strength**: In Chinese culture, black is linked to the element of water, symbolizing power and depth.

African and Indigenous Cultures

- **Connection to Ancestors**: In many African cultures, black is associated with the spiritual realm and ancestral respect.
- **Fertility and Potential**: Black soil is seen as fertile and life-giving, symbolizing growth and renewal.

Black in Nature: Depth and Mystery

Black appears in nature as a symbol of mystery, depth, and contrast:

- **The Night Sky**: The blackness of space represents the infinite and the unknown, inspiring awe and curiosity.
- **Animals**: Black animals, such as ravens and panthers, evoke mystery and power, often featured in folklore and mythology.
- **Volcanic Rock and Soil**: Black volcanic soil is a symbol of fertility and renewal, reflecting its life-giving properties.

The History of Black: Sacred and Subversive

Black's historical significance is deeply intertwined with its associations with power, mystery, and rebellion:

- **Ancient Civilizations**: In Ancient Egypt, black was associated with the fertile soil of the Nile and the god Anubis, symbolizing protection and the afterlife.
- **Medieval Europe**: Black was worn by clergy to symbolize humility and piety but was also feared as a representation of the devil and darkness.
- **The Renaissance**: During the Renaissance, black became a symbol of wealth and authority, as black dyes were expensive and difficult to produce.
- **Modern Era**: In contemporary times, black has become a universal symbol of elegance, sophistication, and individuality.

Black in Art and Fashion

Art

Black has been a critical element in art, symbolizing contrast, depth, and emotion:

- **Baroque Art**: Artists like Caravaggio used black to create dramatic contrasts and evoke intense emotions.
- **Abstract Expressionism**: Artists like Kazimir Malevich and Mark Rothko explored black as a conceptual element, representing infinity and existential questions.

Fashion

Black in fashion is timeless and versatile, symbolizing elegance, authority, and rebellion:

- **Formal Attire**: Black tuxedos and gowns are synonymous with sophistication and high status.
- **Everyday Wear**: Black is a staple in wardrobes for its slimming effect and versatility.
- **Countercultural Statements**: From leather jackets to goth aesthetics, black has long been associated with subcultures and individual expression.

Black in Marketing and Branding

Black is a powerful tool in marketing, often used to convey sophistication, luxury, and authority:

- **Luxury and Exclusivity**: High-end brands like Chanel and Gucci use black to communicate elegance and exclusivity.
- **Simplicity and Minimalism**: Black is often used in minimalist designs to emphasize clarity and focus.
- **Edginess and Rebellion**: Brands targeting younger, trendier audiences use black to symbolize boldness and individuality.

The Role of Black in Everyday Life

Black is a color that commands attention and conveys depth in various aspects of life:

- **Interior Design**: Black accents add contrast and sophistication to spaces but should be balanced to avoid creating a heavy atmosphere.
- **Personal Style**: Wearing black communicates confidence, professionalism, and a sense of timeless style.
- **Workspaces**: Black elements in office design create focus and a professional atmosphere.

Practical Applications of Black
Personal Expression

- **Clothing**: Black garments are versatile, slimming, and suitable for both formal and casual settings.
- **Accessories**: Black watches, bags, and shoes add a touch of elegance and refinement to any outfit.

Home Decor

- **Living Spaces**: Black furniture or decor adds depth and contrast to modern interiors.
- **Kitchens and Bathrooms**: Black accents create a sleek and sophisticated look in these functional spaces.
- **Lighting and Fixtures**: Black metal or matte finishes on fixtures add a contemporary touch.

Events and Celebrations

- **Formal Events**: Black tie attire is the standard for elegant occasions.
- **Thematic Parties**: Black is often used in Halloween or masquerade themes to evoke mystery and drama.

Balancing Black with Other Colors

Black pairs well with a variety of colors, creating striking combinations:

- **Black and White**: A timeless contrast that symbolizes balance and duality.
- **Black and Gold**: Evokes luxury and opulence.
- **Black and Red**: Adds intensity and passion, often used in dramatic designs.

Black in Wellness and Therapy

Black is used in wellness practices to promote grounding and introspection:

- **Grounding Practices**: Black is associated with stability and grounding, making it useful in mindfulness exercises.
- **Focus and Clarity**: Black's neutrality can help create environments conducive to focus and meditation.
- **Protection and Strength**: Black is often used in spiritual practices as a protective color, shielding against negativity.

The Dual Nature of Black

Black's duality lies in its ability to represent both strength and vulnerability, beginnings and endings. It can be both inviting and intimidating, making it one of the most versatile and complex colors.

Conclusion: Embracing the Power of Black

Black is a color of mystery, power, and elegance, capable of evoking profound emotions and commanding attention. By understanding its psychological and symbolic significance, we can use black to create sophisticated environments, express individuality, and explore the depths of our own identity. Whether in art, fashion, or everyday life, black remains a timeless and powerful force.

Chapter 15: Gray: Neutrality, Sophistication, and Ambiguity

Gray is a color of balance and subtlety, existing between the extremes of black and white. It is often associated with neutrality, sophistication, and ambiguity, making it one of the most versatile colors in design, fashion, and art. Gray conveys a sense of calm and control, yet its muted nature can also evoke feelings of detachment or indecision. This chapter explores the psychological, cultural, and historical significance of gray, its role in art and design, and how its understated elegance influences daily life.

The Psychology of Gray: Balance and Complexity

Gray has a unique psychological impact, reflecting neutrality and detachment while offering a sense of stability and sophistication.

Emotional Effects

- **Neutrality and Balance**: Gray represents impartiality and balance, embodying the middle ground between black and white.
- **Sophistication and Elegance**: As a refined and understated color, gray is often associated with professionalism and maturity.
- **Ambiguity and Detachment**: Gray's neutrality can sometimes be perceived as indecision or emotional distance.

Physiological Effects

- **Visual Calm**: Gray is easy on the eyes, providing a sense of calm and reducing visual clutter.
- **Subdued Energy**: Unlike brighter colors, gray does not stimulate strong emotional responses, offering a sense of stability and control.
- **Mood Moderation**: Gray can either balance or suppress energy, depending on its intensity and use in combination with other colors.

The Symbolism of Gray Across Cultures

Gray's meanings are shaped by its position as a neutral color and its association with maturity and formality.

Western Cultures

- **Neutrality and Sophistication**: Gray is often used in professional and corporate settings to convey seriousness and formality.
- **Ambiguity**: In Western thought, gray can symbolize uncertainty or moral ambiguity, as seen in the phrase "gray area."
- **Maturity and Aging**: Gray is linked to wisdom and experience, reflecting the natural graying of hair with age.

Eastern Cultures

- **Detachment and Spirituality**: In some Eastern philosophies, gray represents detachment from material desires and a focus on spiritual growth.
- **Simplicity and Humility**: Gray is associated with modesty and simplicity in traditional Asian aesthetics.

Global Trends

- **Urban Modernity**: Gray is often associated with urban landscapes, representing concrete, steel, and modern architecture.
- **Timelessness**: As a neutral color, gray transcends cultural trends, offering timeless appeal in fashion and design.

Gray in Nature: Subtle Beauty

Gray occurs naturally in various forms, emphasizing its understated beauty and connection to balance:

- **Skies and Clouds**: Overcast skies and clouds evoke feelings of calm or introspection.
- **Rocks and Minerals**: Gray stones, such as granite and slate, symbolize strength and durability.
- **Animals**: Gray wolves, elephants, and doves showcase gray's elegance and adaptability in the natural world.

The History of Gray: From Practicality to Elegance

Gray's historical use reflects its practicality and understated sophistication:

- **Ancient Civilizations**: Gray was used in architecture and tools, symbolizing practicality and strength.
- **Medieval and Renaissance Europe**: Gray was prominent in monastic robes, representing humility and simplicity.
- **Modern Era**: In contemporary times, gray has become synonymous with minimalism and modernity, reflecting a shift toward understated elegance.

Gray in Art and Fashion

Art

Gray has been a critical element in art, offering depth, neutrality, and balance:

- **Classical Art**: Gray was used as a background or shading color to emphasize light and shadow.
- **Modern and Contemporary Art**: Artists like James McNeill Whistler and Gerhard Richter used gray as a primary element to explore emotion and abstraction.

Fashion

Gray in fashion is versatile, symbolizing professionalism, sophistication, and timeless style:

- **Formal Wear**: Gray suits and dresses are staples in business and formal attire, conveying authority and refinement.
- **Casual Elegance**: Lighter shades of gray are popular in casual wear, offering a relaxed yet polished look.
- **Gender Neutrality**: Gray's neutrality makes it a key color in unisex and minimalist fashion trends.

Gray in Marketing and Branding

Gray is widely used in branding to convey professionalism, balance, and modernity:

- **Neutrality and Balance**: Gray provides a neutral base for logos and designs, emphasizing simplicity and clarity.
- **Sophistication**: Luxury brands often use gray to convey elegance and refinement.
- **Technology and Innovation**: Tech companies use gray to represent modernity and reliability, often paired with brighter colors for contrast.

The Role of Gray in Everyday Life

Gray enhances environments and personal expression through its versatility and understated elegance:

- **Interior Design**: Gray walls and furniture create a calm and sophisticated atmosphere, ideal for modern homes and offices.
- **Personal Style**: Wearing gray conveys professionalism, maturity, and a sense of understated confidence.
- **Workspaces**: Gray promotes focus and neutrality in office environments, minimizing distractions.

Practical Applications of Gray
Personal Expression

- **Clothing**: Gray garments are versatile and timeless, suitable for both formal and casual settings.
- **Accessories**: Gray watches, bags, and shoes add a touch of understated elegance to any outfit.

Home Decor

- **Living Spaces**: Gray furniture and decor create a sleek and modern aesthetic.
- **Bedrooms**: Soft gray tones promote relaxation and a sense of tranquility.
- **Bathrooms and Kitchens**: Gray tiles and fixtures emphasize cleanliness and modernity.

Events and Celebrations

- **Corporate Events**: Gray is often used in professional gatherings to convey seriousness and focus.
- **Weddings and Parties**: Gray complements brighter colors, adding balance and sophistication to event decor.

Balancing Gray with Other Colors

Gray pairs beautifully with a range of colors, enhancing its versatility and emotional impact:

- **Gray and White**: A clean, modern combination that emphasizes simplicity and space.
- **Gray and Yellow**: Adds warmth and energy, balancing gray's coolness with yellow's vibrancy.
- **Gray and Blue**: Evokes calmness and sophistication, often used in professional and formal designs.

Gray in Wellness and Therapy

Gray plays a subtle role in wellness practices, promoting balance and neutrality:

- **Mental Focus**: Gray's neutrality creates an environment conducive to focus and reflection.
- **Emotional Stability**: Gray helps moderate intense emotions, offering a calming and grounding effect.
- **Mindfulness**: Soft gray tones in meditation spaces encourage a sense of balance and tranquility.

The Dual Nature of Gray

Gray's duality lies in its ability to represent both stability and ambiguity. While it offers neutrality and calm, excessive use of gray can feel cold or uninspiring. Its versatility allows it to adapt to a wide range of contexts, from minimalist design to luxurious fashion.

Conclusion: Embracing the Sophistication of Gray

Gray is a color of neutrality, sophistication, and subtle elegance. Its understated nature allows it to complement other colors, creating harmonious designs and environments. By understanding its psychological and symbolic significance, we can use gray to foster balance, focus, and timeless style. Whether in art, fashion, or daily life, gray remains a versatile and powerful color of quiet strength.

Chapter 16: Brown: Stability, Grounding, and Comfort

Brown is the color of the earth, symbolizing stability, grounding, and a connection to nature. As a warm and neutral tone, brown evokes feelings of comfort, reliability, and security. Its associations with natural elements like soil, wood, and stone make it a color that embodies practicality and resilience. This chapter explores the psychological, cultural, and historical significance of brown, its applications in art, design, and fashion, and how its earthy qualities influence our lives.

The Psychology of Brown: Grounding and Reassurance

Brown is a deeply grounding color that reflects stability, dependability, and a sense of belonging. Its psychological effects are subtle yet profound.

Emotional Effects

- **Stability and Security**: Brown's connection to the earth evokes feelings of safety, grounding, and permanence.
- **Warmth and Comfort**: Its warm undertones create a cozy and welcoming atmosphere.
- **Practicality and Simplicity**: Brown is often associated with straightforwardness and reliability, symbolizing an unpretentious approach to life.

Physiological Effects

- **Calming Influence**: Brown's neutrality has a calming effect, promoting relaxation and reducing stress.
- **Grounding Sensation**: As a color tied to nature, brown helps anchor the mind, fostering a sense of stability and focus.
- **Visual Subtlety**: Brown's muted tones reduce visual stimulation, creating a sense of balance and harmony.

The Symbolism of Brown Across Cultures

Brown carries a range of meanings across cultures, reflecting its associations with the earth, practicality, and tradition.

Western Cultures

- **Reliability and Humility**: In Western societies, brown represents dependability and modesty, often linked to rural life and traditional values.
- **Nature and Simplicity**: Brown is celebrated as a natural, organic color, representing a back-to-basics lifestyle.
- **Stability and Work Ethic**: Brown is often associated with hard work and endurance, as seen in its connection to farming and craftsmanship.

Eastern Cultures

- **Earth and Grounding**: In many Eastern traditions, brown symbolizes the earth element, representing stability and the foundation of life.
- **Simplicity and Modesty**: Brown is linked to humble living and a connection to nature in Eastern aesthetics.

Global Trends

- **Sustainability and Eco-Consciousness**: Brown has become a symbol of eco-friendliness, often associated with natural and sustainable practices.
- **Tradition and Heritage**: Brown evokes a sense of cultural heritage and timeless values, reflected in its use in traditional crafts and designs.

Brown in Nature: Connection and Resilience

Brown is one of the most prevalent colors in nature, reflecting its role as a foundation of life:

- **Soil and Earth**: Brown soil symbolizes fertility, stability, and the nurturing of life.
- **Wood and Trees**: Brown wood represents strength, growth, and resilience.
- **Animals and Wildlife**: Many animals, such as bears, deer, and owls, use brown as camouflage, reflecting its practicality and adaptability.

The History of Brown: From Utility to Elegance

Brown has played a significant role throughout history, transitioning from a practical color to one of understated elegance:

- **Ancient Civilizations**: Brown pigments, derived from natural clays and minerals, were used in early cave paintings and pottery.
- **Medieval Europe**: Brown was associated with the working class and monks, symbolizing humility and labor.
- **Modern Era**: In contemporary times, brown has been embraced in design and fashion for its warm, organic qualities and its association with sustainability.

Brown in Art and Fashion

Art

Brown has been a foundational color in art, symbolizing earthiness, depth, and realism:

- **Classical Art**: Artists used brown to create depth and texture, often as a base for naturalistic scenes.
- **Renaissance and Baroque Art**: Brown was a key element in chiaroscuro techniques, emphasizing light and shadow.
- **Modern Art**: Contemporary artists use brown to explore themes of nature, heritage, and human connection.

Fashion

Brown in fashion exudes warmth, sophistication, and practicality:

- **Earthy Tones**: Shades like camel, taupe, and chocolate are popular for their versatility and timeless appeal.
- **Casual Wear**: Brown is a staple in casual attire, reflecting comfort and durability.
- **Luxury and Elegance**: Darker browns are used in high-end fashion to convey richness and sophistication.

Brown in Marketing and Branding

Brown is widely used in branding to convey warmth, reliability, and eco-consciousness:

- **Sustainability and Nature**: Brown is often used by brands focusing on organic, natural, and environmentally friendly products.
- **Comfort and Warmth**: Brands like Hershey's and UPS use brown to evoke reliability and approachability.

- **Heritage and Tradition**: Brown is associated with timeless craftsmanship and authenticity, making it a popular choice for artisanal brands.

The Role of Brown in Everyday Life

Brown enhances environments and personal expression by adding warmth, grounding, and a sense of connection to nature:

- **Interior Design**: Brown furniture and accents create a cozy, inviting atmosphere in homes and offices.
- **Personal Style**: Wearing brown conveys practicality, warmth, and a connection to natural elements.
- **Outdoor Spaces**: Brown elements in landscaping, such as wooden structures and soil, blend seamlessly with the environment.

Practical Applications of Brown
Personal Expression

- **Clothing**: Brown garments are versatile and classic, suitable for both casual and formal settings.
- **Accessories**: Leather belts, bags, and shoes in shades of brown add a touch of elegance and durability.

Home Decor

- **Living Spaces**: Wooden furniture and brown accents create a sense of warmth and grounding in communal areas.
- **Kitchens and Dining**: Brown tones in cabinets, countertops, and tableware evoke a natural, wholesome atmosphere.
- **Bedrooms**: Soft brown tones promote relaxation and comfort, ideal for restful environments.

Events and Celebrations

- **Rustic Themes**: Brown is a key color in rustic and earthy event decor, symbolizing tradition and simplicity.
- **Seasonal Celebrations**: Brown is often associated with autumn and Thanksgiving, reflecting the colors of harvest and nature.

Balancing Brown with Other Colors

Brown pairs beautifully with a range of colors, enhancing its warmth and versatility:

- **Brown and Green**: A natural combination that symbolizes growth and harmony.
- **Brown and Blue**: Creates a calming contrast, blending earthiness with serenity.
- **Brown and Gold**: Adds a touch of luxury and sophistication to brown's grounded tones.

Brown in Wellness and Therapy

Brown plays a significant role in wellness practices, promoting grounding and emotional balance:

- **Grounding Practices**: Brown's connection to the earth makes it a powerful color for grounding exercises and mindfulness.
- **Stress Reduction**: Brown tones create a comforting environment, reducing stress and promoting relaxation.
- **Holistic Spaces**: Brown is used in wellness centers and spas to evoke a sense of natural healing and restoration.

The Dual Nature of Brown

Brown's duality lies in its ability to symbolize both stability and simplicity. While it provides grounding and warmth, excessive use of brown can feel monotonous or uninspiring. Balancing brown with other colors and textures ensures it remains dynamic and inviting.

Conclusion: Embracing the Grounded Elegance of Brown

Brown is a color of stability, grounding, and comfort, offering a connection to nature and timeless values. By understanding its psychological and symbolic significance, we can use brown to create warm environments, express practicality and sophistication, and foster a sense of security. Whether in art, fashion, or everyday life, brown remains a steadfast and versatile color that embodies the essence of the earth.

Part 3: Combining Colors for Emotional Impact

Chapter 17: Color Combinations and Their Synergies

Colors rarely exist in isolation; their power lies in how they interact with one another. Color combinations evoke a wide range of emotions, create visual harmony or tension, and communicate complex messages. Understanding how colors work together, their synergies, and their cultural and psychological impacts is key to mastering the language of color. In this chapter, we explore the science of color combinations, their practical applications in design and art, and how they can be used to shape mood, convey meaning, and enhance visual experiences.

The Science of Color Combinations

Color combinations are rooted in the principles of color theory, which is based on the color wheel—a visual representation of colors and their relationships.

Primary, Secondary, and Tertiary Colors

- **Primary Colors**: Red, blue, and yellow are the foundational colors that cannot be created by mixing others.
- **Secondary Colors**: Orange, green, and purple are formed by mixing two primary colors.
- **Tertiary Colors**: These are blends of primary and secondary colors, such as red-orange or blue-green.

Color Harmony

Color harmony refers to aesthetically pleasing color combinations that evoke balance and cohesion:

- **Analogous Colors**: Colors next to each other on the color wheel (e.g., blue, blue-green, and green) create a serene and cohesive look.
- **Complementary Colors**: Colors opposite each other on the wheel (e.g., red and green) create contrast and vibrancy.
- **Triadic Colors**: Three colors evenly spaced around the wheel (e.g., red, yellow, and blue) offer dynamic and balanced compositions.
- **Split-Complementary Colors**: A base color paired with the two adjacent to its complement (e.g., blue with yellow-orange and red-orange) adds complexity while maintaining balance.

Warm and Cool Colors

- **Warm Colors**: Red, orange, and yellow evoke energy, passion, and warmth.
- **Cool Colors**: Blue, green, and purple create calm, tranquility, and introspection.

Psychological and Emotional Impact of Color Combinations

The synergy of colors affects emotions and perceptions, amplifying or balancing their individual psychological effects.

High-Contrast Combinations

- **Impact**: Bold and attention-grabbing, high-contrast combinations like black and white or red and green evoke energy and excitement.
- **Applications**: Used in advertising, sports branding, and dynamic art to create a sense of urgency or drama.

Soft and Subtle Combinations

- **Impact**: Muted combinations like pastel blue and pink or beige and cream create a sense of calm and elegance.
- **Applications**: Popular in interior design and wellness branding to foster relaxation and harmony.

Vibrant Combinations

- **Impact**: Bright and saturated combinations like yellow and purple or orange and teal convey playfulness and creativity.
- **Applications**: Common in fashion, tech branding, and children's products to spark energy and joy.

Monochromatic Schemes

- **Impact**: Variations of a single color, such as different shades of green, evoke simplicity and cohesiveness.
- **Applications**: Used in minimalist designs, professional settings, and art to create a unified and sophisticated aesthetic.

Cultural Significance of Color Combinations

Color combinations hold cultural meanings that vary across regions and traditions. Understanding these associations ensures effective communication and avoids misinterpretation.

Western Cultures

- **Red and Green**: Strongly associated with Christmas, symbolizing joy and festivity.
- **Black and White**: Represents formality and elegance, often used in weddings and formal events.
- **Blue and Yellow**: Evokes cheerfulness and energy, commonly used in branding.

Eastern Cultures

- **Red and Gold**: Associated with prosperity and good fortune, especially in Chinese culture.
- **White and Black**: Linked to mourning and loss in some Asian traditions.
- **Blue and White**: Symbolizes purity and spirituality, often seen in Japanese and Indian art.

Global Trends

- **Earth Tones**: Combinations like brown and green symbolize sustainability and eco-consciousness worldwide.
- **Bright Contrasts**: Combinations like pink and yellow represent inclusivity and modernity in global branding.

Practical Applications of Color Combinations
Art and Design

- **Visual Hierarchy**: Contrasting colors like orange and blue direct attention to key elements in art and design.
- **Depth and Dimension**: Complementary colors like purple and yellow create dynamic depth in paintings and digital art.
- **Mood Setting**: Analogous colors like green and blue foster a tranquil atmosphere in landscapes and designs.

Interior Design

- **Warm and Cozy Spaces**: Warm color combinations like red and orange add energy and intimacy to living areas.
- **Serene Retreats**: Cool combinations like teal and gray create calming and restorative environments in bedrooms and bathrooms.

- **Sophisticated Neutrals**: Neutral palettes with touches of beige, taupe, and ivory offer timeless elegance in professional spaces.

Fashion

- **Bold Statements**: High-contrast combinations like black and red exude confidence and drama.
- **Subtle Elegance**: Monochromatic schemes in soft shades like blush pink or charcoal gray convey understated sophistication.
- **Seasonal Trends**: Bright combinations like coral and mint are popular in spring, while earthy tones like rust and olive dominate autumn fashion.

Marketing and Branding

- **Attention-Grabbing Ads**: Bright complementary colors like yellow and purple create high-energy visuals for promotions.
- **Trust and Reliability**: Blue and white combinations convey professionalism and dependability in financial and healthcare industries.
- **Playful Engagement**: Vibrant palettes like orange and lime green appeal to younger audiences and lifestyle brands.

Common Mistakes in Color Combinations

While color combinations can enhance design and communication, poor choices can undermine their impact:

- **Clashing Colors**: Overly saturated or conflicting colors like neon green and red can feel jarring and chaotic.
- **Overuse of Neutrals**: Excessive reliance on gray or beige may result in a bland and uninspiring design.
- **Ignoring Context**: Failing to consider cultural or emotional associations of color combinations can lead to miscommunication.

Balancing and Enhancing Color Combinations

Achieving harmony in color combinations requires thoughtful balance and the use of complementary design elements:

- **Use Neutrals as Anchors**: Pair bold combinations like red and turquoise with neutrals like gray or white to maintain balance.
- **Incorporate Texture and Patterns**: Add depth and interest to simple combinations like navy and cream by using textured fabrics or patterned designs.

- **Leverage Lighting**: The interplay of natural and artificial light can dramatically influence how colors interact, especially in interior design.

Color Combinations in Wellness and Therapy

Color combinations play a significant role in wellness practices, influencing mood and mental well-being:

- **Healing Spaces**: Cool combinations like lavender and pale blue create a soothing atmosphere in therapy rooms and meditation spaces.
- **Energy Boosts**: Bright combinations like orange and yellow invigorate and energize in gyms or activity spaces.
- **Emotional Balance**: Neutral palettes with earthy tones like taupe and sage promote grounding and stability in wellness centers.

The Dynamic Nature of Color Combinations

Color combinations are dynamic and fluid, capable of transforming spaces, moods, and messages. Their effectiveness lies in the thoughtful integration of individual colors to create a cohesive and meaningful whole.

Conclusion: Mastering the Art of Color Synergy

Color combinations are a powerful tool for communication and expression, shaping how we perceive and interact with the world. By understanding the principles of color theory, cultural contexts, and emotional impacts, we can create harmonious and impactful designs that resonate with diverse audiences. Whether in art, design, fashion, or everyday life, the synergy of colors unlocks endless possibilities for creativity and connection.

Chapter 18: Seasonal Color Palettes and Emotional Shifts

Colors are not static; they interact dynamically with time, weather, and cultural traditions, particularly through the lens of seasons. Seasonal color palettes have long influenced art, fashion, design, and emotional well-being, shaping how we perceive and experience the world throughout the year. In this chapter, we explore the impact of seasonal color palettes, their psychological effects, cultural significance, and applications across various domains.

The Science Behind Seasonal Color Perception

Seasonal color palettes are rooted in nature, as changes in light, weather, and foliage alter how we experience colors:

- **Light and Temperature**: Seasonal shifts in sunlight intensity and hue influence how colors are perceived. Warmer tones dominate in summer, while cooler, muted tones define winter.
- **Nature's Palette**: The natural world provides inspiration, from the vibrant blossoms of spring to the earthy hues of autumn leaves.
- **Psychological Cycles**: Our emotional state fluctuates with seasons, influencing how we respond to different colors.

Seasonal Color Palettes and Their Emotional Impact

Each season evokes specific emotional responses, guided by its characteristic colors and cultural associations.

Spring: Renewal and Growth

Spring represents renewal, growth, and optimism, reflected in its light and fresh color palette.

- **Color Palette**: Soft pastels like blush pink, mint green, lavender, and baby blue.
- **Emotional Impact**:
  - **Positivity and Energy**: Light, airy colors evoke feelings of hope and new beginnings.
  - **Rejuvenation**: Green tones symbolize growth and vitality, mirroring the budding of plants.
- **Applications**:
  - **Interior Design**: Spring palettes brighten living spaces, promoting energy and freshness.
  - **Fashion**: Pastel clothing reflects the lightheartedness of the season.

Summer: Vibrancy and Energy

Summer is marked by energy, warmth, and abundance, mirrored in its vibrant and saturated colors.

- **Color Palette**: Bold hues like sunny yellow, coral, turquoise, and hot pink.
- **Emotional Impact**:
  - **Excitement and Joy**: Bright, saturated colors stimulate enthusiasm and social engagement.
  - **Energy Boost**: Warm tones like orange and red evoke heat and vitality.
- **Applications**:
  - **Events and Celebrations**: Summer palettes dominate beach parties, weddings, and festivals.
  - **Marketing**: Bright colors in advertisements grab attention and convey fun and spontaneity.

Autumn: Warmth and Reflection

Autumn's rich, earthy tones evoke warmth, nostalgia, and introspection.

- **Color Palette**: Deep shades like rust, mustard, olive green, and burgundy.
- **Emotional Impact**:
  - **Comfort and Grounding**: Warm, muted tones create a sense of coziness and security.
  - **Reflection**: Earthy colors encourage introspection, aligning with the season's slowing pace.
- **Applications**:
  - **Interior Design**: Autumn palettes feature in rustic decor, evoking warmth and comfort.
  - **Fashion**: Sweaters and scarves in earthy tones dominate fall wardrobes.

Winter: Stillness and Elegance

Winter is characterized by cool, crisp tones and an understated elegance.

- **Color Palette**: Icy blues, deep navy, silver, white, and rich jewel tones like emerald and ruby.
- **Emotional Impact**:
  - **Calm and Focus**: Cool tones evoke tranquility and clarity, aligning with the stillness of winter.
  - **Sophistication**: Jewel tones and metallics convey luxury and celebration.
- **Applications**:
  - **Holiday Decor**: Winter palettes feature prominently in holiday designs, from snowy whites to festive reds.
  - **Art and Fashion**: Winter-inspired art and clothing emphasize elegance and richness.

Cultural Significance of Seasonal Color Palettes

Seasonal colors hold different meanings across cultures, reflecting local traditions and climates.

Western Cultures

- **Spring**: Associated with Easter and renewal, marked by pastel colors.
- **Summer**: Linked to holidays and outdoor activities, characterized by vibrant hues.
- **Autumn**: Evokes harvest and Thanksgiving, dominated by warm, earthy tones.
- **Winter**: Celebrates Christmas and New Year, featuring reds, greens, and metallics.

Eastern Cultures

- **Spring**: Celebrated with cherry blossoms in Japan, symbolized by pale pink and white.
- **Summer**: Festivals often feature bright and bold colors, emphasizing vitality.
- **Autumn**: Harvest celebrations incorporate golds, reds, and browns.
- **Winter**: Cool blues and whites reflect snow and tranquility, often paired with reds for Lunar New Year.

Global Trends

- **Eco-Seasonal Colors**: With growing environmental awareness, seasonal palettes now emphasize sustainability, featuring organic and muted tones that mimic natural materials.

Seasonal Color Palettes in Art and Design

Art

- **Seasonal Inspirations**: Artists like Monet captured the changing seasons through color, showcasing how light and nature influence perception.
- **Thematic Art**: Seasonal themes, such as winter landscapes or autumn forests, evoke specific emotions tied to the time of year.

Interior Design

- **Seasonal Decor**: Rotating decor with seasonal colors keeps spaces fresh and reflective of the time of year.
- **Mood Enhancement**: Spring palettes uplift, summer palettes energize, autumn palettes ground, and winter palettes calm.

Fashion

- **Seasonal Trends**: Designers align collections with seasonal palettes, using light fabrics and pastels in spring and heavier, richer colors in winter.

• **Timeless vs. Seasonal**: While some colors remain timeless, integrating seasonal hues adds relevance and vibrancy to wardrobes.

Seasonal Color Palettes in Marketing and Branding

Seasonal colors are powerful tools for marketing, influencing consumer behavior and enhancing brand identity:

• **Spring Campaigns**: Soft colors convey freshness and renewal, ideal for promoting new products or services.
• **Summer Promotions**: Bright palettes evoke energy and excitement, perfect for travel and leisure branding.
• **Autumn Sales**: Warm, earthy tones create nostalgia, encouraging purchases during harvest festivals or back-to-school campaigns.
• **Winter Holidays**: Jewel tones and metallics evoke luxury and festivity, aligning with gift-giving seasons.

Psychological Shifts with Seasonal Colors

Colors not only reflect the seasons but also influence how we feel during different times of the year:

• **Seasonal Affective Disorder (SAD)**: Incorporating brighter colors during darker months can help alleviate mood dips.
• **Energy Regulation**: Cool colors in summer promote relaxation, while warm tones in winter create a sense of coziness.
• **Creativity and Productivity**: Seasonal colors can inspire creativity and adjust productivity levels, making them valuable in workspace design.

Practical Tips for Using Seasonal Color Palettes
Home Decor

- Rotate soft furnishings like cushions, curtains, and rugs to reflect seasonal colors.
- Use neutral bases (e.g., white walls) to allow for easy integration of seasonal accents.

Fashion

- Invest in versatile wardrobe staples in neutral tones, accented by seasonal colors through accessories or statement pieces.
- Layer seasonal palettes for transitional periods, like late autumn or early spring.

Marketing

- Update branding materials, including websites and social media, to align with seasonal themes.
- Use seasonal colors strategically in product packaging to increase relevance and appeal.

The Timeless Appeal of Seasonal Color Palettes

Seasonal color palettes offer a cyclical rhythm that resonates with nature, emotions, and cultural traditions. Their ability to evoke specific feelings and memories makes them indispensable in art, design, and personal expression.

Conclusion: Harnessing the Power of Seasonal Colors

Seasonal color palettes reflect the natural world's rhythms, influencing our moods, behaviors, and creativity. By understanding the emotional and cultural significance of these palettes, we can align our environments, clothing, and designs with the seasons, fostering harmony and resonance throughout the year. Whether through art, fashion, or marketing, the thoughtful use of seasonal colors brings life and relevance to every moment.

Chapter 19: Colors in Art and Design: Communicating Emotion

Colors are a fundamental element in art and design, serving as a powerful tool to communicate emotion, evoke reactions, and create visual impact. The strategic use of color transcends language and cultural barriers, influencing how we perceive and interpret the world. In this chapter, we delve into the role of color in art and design, examining its psychological effects, cultural symbolism, and practical applications in various artistic and creative disciplines.

The Emotional Power of Color in Art and Design

Color is deeply tied to human emotion, acting as a catalyst for feelings and reactions. Different colors evoke specific emotional responses, often subconsciously, making them a critical element in visual communication.

Psychological Effects of Colors

- **Warm Colors (Red, Orange, Yellow):**
    - **Red**: Evokes passion, urgency, or danger.
    - **Orange**: Inspires energy, enthusiasm, and creativity.
    - **Yellow**: Promotes happiness, optimism, and clarity.
- **Cool Colors (Blue, Green, Purple):**
    - **Blue**: Conveys calmness, trust, and introspection.
    - **Green**: Symbolizes growth, balance, and renewal.
    - **Purple**: Represents imagination, spirituality, and luxury.
- **Neutral Colors (Black, White, Gray, Brown):**
    - **Black**: Suggests power, elegance, or mystery.
    - **White**: Evokes purity, simplicity, and new beginnings.
    - **Gray**: Implies sophistication, neutrality, and ambiguity.
    - **Brown**: Conveys stability, grounding, and comfort.

Emotional Amplification Through Color

- Artists and designers use color combinations to amplify or contrast emotions. For example:
    - **Red and Black**: Creates tension and drama.
    - **Blue and White**: Evokes serenity and peace.
    - **Yellow and Gray**: Balances cheerfulness with sophistication.

The Role of Color in Artistic Movements

Throughout history, artists have used color to define movements, communicate ideas, and challenge societal norms.

Impressionism

- **Focus on Light and Color**: Impressionist painters like Claude Monet used light, pastel, and natural colors to capture fleeting moments.
- **Emotional Impact**: The use of soft, vibrant palettes created a sense of optimism and immediacy.

Expressionism

- **Bold and Intense Colors**: Artists like Edvard Munch used stark contrasts and exaggerated hues to convey inner turmoil and raw emotion.
- **Psychological Depth**: Colors were chosen for their emotional rather than realistic qualities.

Abstract Expressionism

- **Emphasis on Emotion**: Painters like Mark Rothko used large fields of color to evoke emotional introspection and spiritual experiences.
- **Simplified Palettes**: Limited colors were used to focus on mood and texture.

Pop Art

- **Vivid Colors**: Bright, saturated colors in works by Andy Warhol reflected consumerism and mass culture.
- **Playful Emotion**: Bold palettes captured energy and the irreverence of the modern era.

Color in Design: From Branding to User Experience

Designers use color intentionally to influence perception, enhance usability, and create memorable experiences.

Brand Identity

- **Emotional Branding**: Colors are chosen to align with a brand's message:
  - **Red**: Coca-Cola's energy and passion.
  - **Blue**: Facebook's reliability and trust.
  - **Green**: Starbucks' sustainability and growth.
- **Differentiation**: Unique color schemes help brands stand out in crowded markets.

User Interface (UI) and User Experience (UX) Design

- **Guiding Attention**: High-contrast colors direct users to important elements, such as buttons or calls-to-action.
- **Creating Hierarchy**: Color gradients and variations distinguish content levels and priorities.
- **Enhancing Accessibility**: Thoughtful color choices improve readability and navigation for users with visual impairments.

Interior Design

- **Mood Creation**: Colors define the atmosphere of a space:
    - **Warm tones** energize social spaces.
    - **Cool tones** calm bedrooms or relaxation areas.
- **Spatial Illusion**: Light colors make rooms feel larger, while dark tones create intimacy.

Cultural Symbolism of Color in Art and Design

Color symbolism varies across cultures, shaping how colors are interpreted in different contexts.

Western Cultures

- **White**: Associated with purity and weddings.
- **Black**: Linked to mourning and sophistication.
- **Red**: Evokes love or danger.

Eastern Cultures

- **Red**: Symbolizes luck and prosperity in Chinese culture.
- **White**: Represents mourning and death in many Asian traditions.
- **Gold**: Associated with wealth and divine power.

Global Design Trends

- Designers working internationally consider cultural symbolism to ensure color choices resonate appropriately with diverse audiences.

Techniques for Using Color in Art and Design
Contrast and Balance

- **High Contrast**: Adds drama and ensures readability (e.g., white text on a black background).
- **Low Contrast**: Creates harmony and subtlety (e.g., pastel combinations).

Color Gradients

- Gradients add depth and dimension, transitioning between shades to create smooth visual flows.

Monochromatic Schemes

- Using variations of a single hue emphasizes simplicity and cohesion.

Complementary Colors

- Pairing opposites on the color wheel creates dynamic and striking visuals.

Analogous Colors

- Adjacent colors on the wheel create harmonious and cohesive designs.

Practical Applications of Color in Art and Design
Fine Art

- **Emotional Resonance**: Artists use color to connect with viewers on a visceral level.
- **Narrative and Symbolism**: Colors tell stories or highlight thematic elements.

Graphic Design

- **Visual Branding**: Colors establish identity and evoke emotions associated with a company or product.
- **Communication**: Infographics use color to convey information quickly and effectively.

Fashion Design

- **Seasonal Trends**: Designers align collections with seasonal palettes to reflect cultural and environmental influences.
- **Mood Expression**: Clothing colors convey mood, from the bold energy of red to the serenity of blue.

Photography

- **Color Grading**: Photographers manipulate tones to evoke nostalgia, drama, or intimacy.
- **Natural Lighting**: Harnessing natural light enhances color vibrancy and authenticity.

Challenges in Using Color to Communicate Emotion
Overuse of Bright Colors

- Too many vivid tones can overwhelm viewers, diminishing the intended emotional impact.

Cultural Misinterpretation

- Failing to consider cultural symbolism can result in unintended messaging.

Inconsistent Application

- Inconsistent use of colors across mediums or platforms can dilute a brand's identity or artistic vision.

The Future of Color in Art and Design
Digital Innovation

- Advances in digital tools allow for precise color manipulation, enhancing creative possibilities.
- Virtual and augmented reality experiences increasingly rely on color to immerse users in digital environments.

Sustainability and Natural Palettes

- As sustainability becomes a priority, designers are shifting toward earthy, natural tones to reflect eco-conscious values.

Dynamic Color Systems

- Adaptive designs, where colors change based on user input or environmental conditions, are becoming more prevalent.

Conclusion: The Emotional Language of Color in Art and Design

Colors are more than visual elements; they are a language that conveys emotion, shapes perception, and creates meaning. By understanding the psychological and cultural impact of color, artists and designers can craft powerful, resonant works that connect with their audiences on a deeper level. Whether in fine art, branding, or user experience, the strategic use of color is essential for effective communication and emotional engagement.

Part 4: Applying Color Codes in Everyday Life

Chapter 20: Colors in Your Environment: Home and Workspaces

The colors in our environments—both at home and at work—significantly influence our emotions, productivity, and overall well-being. Thoughtful color choices can create harmony, foster creativity, reduce stress, and even enhance focus. In this chapter, we explore the psychological impact of color in various settings, practical tips for incorporating color into home and workspaces, and how to adapt color schemes to suit specific needs and personal preferences.

The Psychology of Color in Environmental Design

Colors have a direct impact on how we feel and behave in a space. Understanding these effects is crucial when designing environments that support our goals and well-being.

Warm Colors

- **Red**: Energizes and stimulates, but overuse can cause feelings of agitation or stress. Ideal for dynamic areas like kitchens or gyms.
- **Orange**: Encourages social interaction and creativity, making it suitable for living rooms or collaborative workspaces.
- **Yellow**: Promotes positivity and focus, great for kitchens, playrooms, or work areas, but should be used sparingly to avoid overstimulation.

Cool Colors

- **Blue**: Calms and soothes, perfect for bedrooms, bathrooms, or offices where focus and tranquility are needed.
- **Green**: Represents balance and renewal, ideal for living spaces, offices, and places of relaxation.
- **Purple**: Evokes imagination and spirituality. Light shades work well in bedrooms, while darker tones add elegance to living areas.

Neutral Colors

- **White**: Enhances openness and cleanliness, great for minimalist designs, but can feel sterile without complementary accents.
- **Gray**: Conveys sophistication and neutrality, versatile for modern homes and offices.
- **Brown**: Offers warmth and grounding, suitable for rustic or traditional designs.

Bold and Dark Colors

- **Black**: Adds depth and sophistication but should be used sparingly to avoid a heavy or oppressive feel.
- **Jewel Tones**: Deep colors like emerald green or sapphire blue create a luxurious atmosphere.

Designing Color Schemes for Home Environments
Living Rooms

- **Purpose**: Socializing, relaxation, or entertainment.
- **Recommended Colors**:
    ◦ Warm tones (yellow, orange) for sociability.
    ◦ Cool tones (blue, green) for relaxation.
    ◦ Neutral tones (beige, taupe) for versatility.
- **Tips**:
    ◦ Use accent walls or colorful furnishings to introduce vibrancy.
    ◦ Incorporate natural light to enhance the chosen palette.

Bedrooms

- **Purpose**: Rest and relaxation.
- **Recommended Colors**:
    ◦ Cool tones (blue, lavender) for calmness.
    ◦ Warm, muted tones (peach, blush pink) for coziness.
- **Tips**:
    ◦ Avoid bright, stimulating colors like red or orange.
    ◦ Use soft lighting to complement the restful ambiance.

Kitchens and Dining Areas

- **Purpose**: Cooking, eating, and gathering.
- **Recommended Colors**:
    ◦ Warm tones (red, yellow) to stimulate appetite and conversation.
    ◦ Neutral tones (white, gray) for a clean, modern look.
- **Tips**:
    ◦ Use colorful backsplashes or utensils for subtle pops of color.
    ◦ Balance bold colors with neutral countertops or cabinetry.

Bathrooms

- **Purpose**: Hygiene and relaxation.
- **Recommended Colors**:
    ◦ Cool tones (blue, teal) for a spa-like feel.
    ◦ Neutral tones (white, beige) for cleanliness.
- **Tips**:
    ◦ Add green accents, such as plants, for a natural touch.

• Use soft, diffused lighting to enhance the calming palette.

Home Offices

- **Purpose**: Productivity and focus.
- **Recommended Colors**:
    - Blue for focus and efficiency.
    - Green for balance and creativity.
    - Yellow accents for energy and clarity.
- **Tips**:
    - Limit bright colors to accent pieces to avoid distractions.
    - Use adjustable lighting to adapt to different tasks.

Children's Rooms

- **Purpose**: Play, learning, and rest.
- **Recommended Colors**:
    - Bright, playful tones (yellow, orange) for energy and joy.
    - Pastels (light pink, mint green) for calming and nurturing.
- **Tips**:
    - Incorporate murals or decals for flexibility as the child grows.
    - Avoid overstimulating colors, particularly near sleeping areas.

Designing Color Schemes for Workspaces
Corporate Offices

- **Purpose**: Collaboration, productivity, and professionalism.
- **Recommended Colors**:
    - Blue for trust and focus.
    - Green for creativity and stress reduction.
    - Gray and white for neutrality and modernity.
- **Tips**:
    - Introduce accent colors in meeting rooms to inspire creativity.
    - Use ergonomic furniture with complementary tones to enhance comfort.

Creative Studios

- **Purpose**: Innovation and artistic expression.
- **Recommended Colors**:
    - Bright, energizing tones (orange, turquoise) to inspire creativity.
    - Neutral backgrounds (white, beige) to avoid overwhelming the senses.
- **Tips**:
    - Allow for adaptable lighting to highlight different areas of the studio.
    - Incorporate personal artwork or decor to reflect individual style.

Retail and Client-Facing Spaces

- **Purpose**: Attracting customers, fostering trust, and promoting sales.
- **Recommended Colors**:
    - Red or orange for urgency and energy in promotional areas.
    - Green for organic or eco-friendly brands.
    - Neutral tones for high-end or minimalist aesthetics.
- **Tips**:
    - Ensure consistency with brand colors to reinforce identity.
    - Use lighting strategically to accentuate key displays.

Remote Workspaces

- **Purpose**: Flexibility, focus, and comfort.
- **Recommended Colors**:
  - Blue and green for calmness and productivity.
  - Soft yellows for energy in small doses.
- **Tips**:
  - Add personal touches like plants or artwork for warmth.
  - Opt for adjustable standing desks or chairs with neutral finishes.

Incorporating Seasonal Color Changes

Refreshing color schemes to reflect seasonal changes can invigorate both home and work environments:

- **Spring**: Add pastel tones and floral accents for renewal.
- **Summer**: Incorporate bright, sunny hues like coral or turquoise.
- **Autumn**: Use warm, earthy tones like rust and mustard.
- **Winter**: Emphasize cool tones like icy blue or deep jewel tones for elegance.

Practical Tips for Color Integration
Layering Colors

- Use a base color for walls and larger furniture.
- Add complementary or contrasting accent colors through cushions, rugs, or art.

Using Textures

- Incorporate textured materials like wood, stone, or fabric to add depth and interest to monochromatic schemes.

Lighting Considerations

- Natural light enhances warm and cool tones differently. Test colors in various lighting conditions.
- Use layered lighting (ambient, task, and accent) to adapt to different needs.

Plants and Natural Elements

- Greenery complements any color scheme, bringing a sense of vitality and harmony.

Common Mistakes to Avoid

- **Overusing Bright Colors**: Excessive vibrancy can cause overstimulation and fatigue.
- **Ignoring Light Conditions**: Colors may appear differently under artificial versus natural light.
- **Mismatch with Function**: Choosing colors that clash with a room's purpose can reduce comfort and usability.
- **Too Many Colors**: Overcomplicating palettes can make spaces feel chaotic.

The Emotional Benefits of Thoughtful Color Design

The right color choices in home and work environments offer tangible emotional and psychological benefits:

- **Enhanced Mood**: Cheerful tones can elevate spirits, while calming hues reduce stress.
- **Improved Focus**: Cool, neutral palettes create an atmosphere of concentration.
- **Increased Creativity**: Bold and playful colors stimulate innovative thinking.
- **Better Sleep**: Restful palettes in bedrooms support healthy sleep patterns.

Conclusion: Harnessing the Power of Color in Environments

Colors in home and workspaces play a pivotal role in shaping our daily lives, influencing emotions, productivity, and well-being. By thoughtfully selecting and combining colors, we can create environments that are not only visually appealing but also aligned with our functional and emotional needs. Whether through bold statements, subtle accents, or seasonal refreshes, color is a versatile tool that transforms the spaces where we live and work.

Chapter 21: Dressing in Color: What Your Wardrobe Says About You
Clothing is one of the most immediate and powerful forms of self-expression, and color plays a significant role in shaping how we perceive ourselves and how others perceive us. The colors we wear can communicate confidence, authority, creativity, and even mood, making our wardrobe a canvas for personal identity. This chapter explores the psychology of clothing colors, their cultural significance, and how to use color strategically to reflect your personality, enhance your appearance, and align with different occasions.

The Psychology of Clothing Colors
The colors in your wardrobe have a profound impact on how you feel and how others respond to you. Each color carries unique psychological connotations that can shape perceptions and emotions.

Warm Colors

- **Red**: Conveys confidence, power, and passion. Red outfits command attention and are often worn to make bold statements.
- **Orange**: Represents energy, enthusiasm, and warmth. It's a playful color that invites approachability and friendliness.
- **Yellow**: Evokes optimism, creativity, and cheerfulness. Yellow is a great choice for social or creative settings but should be used sparingly to avoid overwhelming others.

Cool Colors

- **Blue**: Symbolizes calmness, trust, and dependability. Blue is a favorite for professional attire, signaling reliability and composure.
- **Green**: Reflects balance, growth, and vitality. Green is ideal for conveying harmony and eco-consciousness.
- **Purple**: Suggests creativity, luxury, and spirituality. Purple is a striking color that can add an air of sophistication or whimsy.

Neutral Colors

- **White**: Represents purity, simplicity, and clarity. White outfits exude freshness and elegance, often chosen for formal or minimalist looks.
- **Gray**: Conveys sophistication, neutrality, and balance. Gray is versatile, offering a polished yet understated appeal.
- **Black**: Evokes power, elegance, and mystery. Black is a timeless choice for creating a commanding presence or a sleek, stylish look.

- **Brown**: Symbolizes stability, warmth, and practicality. Brown outfits are grounding and convey a sense of reliability.

The Cultural Significance of Clothing Colors

Color associations vary widely across cultures, influencing how clothing colors are interpreted in different contexts.

Western Cultures

- **Red**: Associated with love and passion, often worn on romantic occasions or for bold fashion statements.
- **Black**: Symbolizes elegance and formality but is also linked to mourning.
- **White**: Represents purity, making it a traditional choice for weddings and celebrations.

Eastern Cultures

- **Red**: A color of luck and prosperity, commonly worn during celebrations like weddings or Lunar New Year.
- **White**: Often associated with mourning and funerals in many Asian cultures.
- **Gold**: Represents wealth, success, and divine power.

Global Trends

- **Earth Tones**: Brown, beige, and olive green have gained popularity worldwide, reflecting sustainability and connection to nature.
- **Bright Contrasts**: Vibrant color combinations symbolize modernity and cultural fusion in global fashion.

Dressing for Mood and Personality

The colors you wear can reflect your mood, boost confidence, or showcase your personality. Here's how to align your wardrobe with your emotional and personal expression.

Expressing Mood

- **Confidence**: Wear red, black, or jewel tones like emerald green or sapphire blue to exude authority and self-assurance.
- **Creativity**: Opt for bright colors like orange, turquoise, or fuchsia to highlight your artistic side.
- **Calm and Relaxation**: Choose cool tones like light blue, lavender, or mint green for a serene and composed look.

Showcasing Personality

- **Bold and Adventurous**: Bright, contrasting colors and unique patterns reflect a daring and outgoing nature.
- **Classic and Timeless**: Neutral palettes with whites, blacks, grays, and beige convey sophistication and a preference for tradition.
- **Earthy and Grounded**: Warm tones like rust, olive, and mustard showcase a connection to nature and practicality.

Using Color to Enhance Your Appearance
Colors can complement your skin tone, hair color, and eye color, enhancing your natural beauty.
Skin Tones

- **Warm Undertones**: Earthy colors like olive, coral, and gold enhance warm skin tones.
- **Cool Undertones**: Jewel tones like sapphire, emerald, and lavender bring out the best in cool skin tones.
- **Neutral Undertones**: Versatile shades like blush pink, light gray, and navy work well for neutral skin tones.

Hair Colors

- **Blonde**: Pastels, white, and navy provide a striking contrast.
- **Brunette**: Jewel tones and warm earth colors enhance richness.
- **Red Hair**: Green, teal, and rust create a complementary look.

Eye Colors

- **Blue Eyes**: Shades of blue, gray, and soft browns make eyes pop.
- **Green Eyes**: Purple, burgundy, and moss green create a vivid contrast.
- **Brown Eyes**: Warm colors like copper, gold, and bronze highlight depth.

Dressing for Occasions: Color Strategies
Formal Events

- Black-tie occasions call for elegant colors like black, navy, or deep burgundy.
- Lighter shades like ivory or pale gray can add sophistication for daytime formal events.

Professional Settings

- Neutral tones like navy, gray, and beige convey reliability and professionalism.
- Add a pop of color, such as a red tie or pastel blouse, to showcase personality without over-powering.

Social Gatherings

- Bright and playful colors like coral, turquoise, or yellow foster a welcoming atmosphere.
- Patterns or bold accessories can create conversation starters.

Romantic Dates

- Red or pink conveys passion and warmth.
- Softer tones like blush or lavender suggest tenderness and approachability.

Casual Outings

- Earthy tones like khaki, olive, and light denim are relaxed and practical.
- Bright accents add personality to casual looks.

Building a Versatile Wardrobe with Color

A well-rounded wardrobe incorporates a range of colors to suit different moods, occasions, and styles.

Essential Neutrals

- Invest in classic pieces in black, white, navy, and gray as the foundation of your wardrobe.
- These colors provide versatility and can be paired with any accent color.

Seasonal Pops

- Rotate brighter or seasonal colors like pastels in spring, bold tones in summer, warm hues in autumn, and jewel tones in winter.

Statement Pieces

- Include a few standout items in vibrant colors or patterns that express your unique personality.

Accessories

- Use scarves, ties, shoes, and jewelry to introduce colors without overwhelming your outfit.

Common Mistakes and How to Avoid Them

- **Overusing Bright Colors**: Too many vibrant tones can clash. Pair bold colors with neutrals for balance.
- **Ignoring Skin Tone**: Wearing colors that don't complement your natural tones can wash you out or overpower your look.
- **Mismatch with Occasion**: Wearing overly casual or formal colors can make you feel out of place.

The Future of Color in Fashion

- **Technology and Wearable Trends**: Color-changing fabrics and smart textiles are emerging, allowing for adaptive fashion.
- **Sustainability**: Earthy, natural tones and eco-friendly dyes are gaining prominence in response to environmental concerns.
- **Inclusivity**: Fashion brands are embracing a broader spectrum of colors to cater to diverse cultural and personal identities.

Conclusion: Dressing with Color to Reflect Who You Are

Your wardrobe is a powerful form of self-expression, and the colors you wear are a statement about your mood, personality, and style. By understanding the psychological and cultural impact of clothing colors, you can curate a wardrobe that not only enhances your appearance but also communicates your individuality and aligns with your life's occasions. Dressing in color is an art that blends personal expression with practical considerations, offering endless opportunities for creativity and connection.

Chapter 22: Marketing and Branding: Using Colors to Influence Behavior

Color is a critical component of marketing and branding, serving as a visual cue that communicates identity, evokes emotion, and influences consumer behavior. Companies strategically use color to make their brands memorable, attract specific audiences, and inspire action. This chapter explores the psychology of color in marketing, its cultural implications, and practical strategies for using color to influence behavior and achieve branding goals.

The Psychology of Color in Marketing

Colors influence how people perceive a brand, product, or service. They evoke emotions and behaviors that can drive purchasing decisions.

How Colors Affect Emotions

- **Red**: Evokes urgency, passion, and excitement. Often used in sales promotions and fast-food branding to stimulate appetite and impulse buying.
- **Blue**: Conveys trust, dependability, and professionalism. Common in financial institutions and technology brands.
- **Green**: Represents nature, health, and growth. Used by brands focused on sustainability, wellness, or finance.
- **Yellow**: Suggests optimism, energy, and attention. Effective for grabbing attention in advertisements or signage.
- **Purple**: Symbolizes luxury, creativity, and spirituality. Favored by high-end or imaginative brands.
- **Black**: Denotes sophistication, elegance, and power. Widely used in luxury branding.
- **White**: Reflects simplicity, cleanliness, and modernity. Popular in minimalist and health-related brands.

Color and Consumer Behavior

- **Impulse Shoppers**: Respond to bold, warm colors like red, orange, and black.
- **Budget-Conscious Shoppers**: Prefer blue and green, which convey trust and security.
- **Luxury Buyers**: Are drawn to black, gold, and deep jewel tones, which signal exclusivity and refinement.

The Role of Color in Branding
Colors play a vital role in establishing brand identity, differentiation, and emotional resonance.
Establishing Brand Identity

- Colors act as visual shorthand for a brand's values and personality. For example:
    - **Coca-Cola (Red)**: Passionate, energetic, and bold.
    - **Facebook (Blue)**: Trustworthy, social, and calming.
    - **Starbucks (Green)**: Natural, sustainable, and fresh.

Differentiation

- Unique color schemes help brands stand out in competitive markets. Example:
    - **Tiffany & Co. (Robin's Egg Blue)**: Instantly recognizable and synonymous with luxury and exclusivity.

Building Emotional Connections

- Colors foster emotional bonds with consumers. For instance:
    - **Red Bull (Red and Blue)**: Combines energy and reliability to align with its adventurous, youthful audience.
    - **Whole Foods (Green and White)**: Reflects health and environmental responsibility.

Color in Marketing Materials
Logos

- Logos are often a brand's first visual impression. The color of a logo should encapsulate the brand's essence:
    - **Nike (Black)**: Power and simplicity.
    - **McDonald's (Red and Yellow)**: Energy and cheerfulness.
    - **Spotify (Green)**: Freshness and growth.

Packaging

- Packaging colors influence buying decisions:
    - **Bright Colors**: Attract attention on shelves and are often used for snack foods or children's products.
    - **Earthy Tones**: Convey eco-friendliness and natural ingredients, popular with organic brands.
    - **Metallics**: Signal luxury and premium quality, common in cosmetics and electronics.

Advertisements

- **Warm Colors**: Create a sense of urgency and are effective for limited-time offers.
- **Cool Colors**: Promote relaxation and trust, ideal for service-based advertisements.
- **Neutral Colors**: Provide balance and professionalism, often used in B2B marketing.

Web Design

- **Call-to-Action (CTA) Buttons**: Bright colors like red, orange, or green encourage clicks.
- **Backgrounds**: Neutral or subtle tones ensure text and visuals stand out.
- **Navigation**: Consistent use of brand colors enhances user experience and reinforces brand identity.

Cultural Implications of Color in Marketing
Color meanings vary across cultures, requiring global brands to adapt their color strategies.
Western Cultures

- **Red**: Passion and urgency (sales, romance).
- **Blue**: Trust and professionalism (finance, tech).
- **White**: Cleanliness and purity (health, weddings).

Eastern Cultures

- **Red**: Luck and prosperity (festivals, celebrations).
- **White**: Mourning and death (funerals).
- **Gold**: Wealth and success (luxury brands).

Middle Eastern Cultures

- **Green**: Sacredness and peace (religious significance).
- **Black**: Elegance and power, but also mourning.
- **White**: Purity and spirituality.

Latin American Cultures

- **Bright Colors**: Vibrancy and joy, reflecting cultural dynamism.
- **Yellow**: Associated with wealth and energy.
- **Black**: Power but also mourning.

Using Color to Drive Behavior
Brands can use color to evoke specific actions and responses from consumers.
Stimulating Purchases

- Red and orange create a sense of urgency, effective for flash sales or limited-time offers.
- Yellow grabs attention and encourages impulse buys.

Fostering Loyalty

- Blue builds trust and reliability, making it ideal for loyalty programs or subscription services.
- Green promotes ethical practices, appealing to eco-conscious consumers.

Enhancing Perceived Value

- Black and gold elevate a product's perceived worth, often used in luxury branding.
- White packaging suggests simplicity and high quality, particularly in beauty and tech products.

Encouraging Exploration

- Bright, playful colors like pink and turquoise attract younger audiences, encouraging them to engage with interactive or experiential campaigns.

Case Studies: Successful Use of Color in Marketing
Apple

- **Color Strategy**: White and silver dominate, reflecting modernity, simplicity, and innovation.
- **Impact**: Reinforces a clean, user-friendly brand image and aligns with premium pricing.

Target

- **Color Strategy**: Bold red conveys energy and urgency, making the brand memorable.
- **Impact**: Creates an approachable yet dynamic retail experience, encouraging impulse buys.

Starbucks

- **Color Strategy**: Green symbolizes sustainability and freshness, aligning with the company's mission.
- **Impact**: Cultivates a connection with environmentally conscious customers.

Lego

- **Color Strategy**: Bright primary colors (red, yellow, blue) evoke fun, creativity, and nostalgia.
- **Impact**: Appeals to children and adults alike, fostering brand loyalty across generations.

Practical Tips for Using Color in Marketing

1. **Define Your Brand Personality**: Choose colors that align with your brand's core values and target audience.
2. **Test Your Audience's Preferences**: Conduct A/B testing with different color schemes to determine what resonates most.
3. **Consider Cultural Sensitivities**: Adapt color choices for global markets to ensure they align with local symbolism.
4. **Create Contrast**: Use contrasting colors to make key elements like logos or CTA buttons stand out.
5. **Be Consistent**: Maintain a cohesive color palette across all platforms to reinforce brand recognition.

The Future of Color in Marketing
Dynamic and Adaptive Colors

- AI-driven platforms allow colors to adapt to user preferences or environmental factors, creating personalized experiences.

Augmented Reality (AR) and Virtual Reality (VR)

- Immersive technologies use color to enhance interactivity and deepen emotional engagement.

Sustainable Branding

- Eco-friendly brands are increasingly using natural, muted palettes to communicate their commitment to sustainability.

Inclusivity in Color Choices

- Brands are expanding their palettes to reflect diversity and inclusivity, appealing to broader demographics.

Conclusion: Mastering the Art of Color in Marketing and Branding
Color is a powerful, multifaceted tool that influences perception, emotion, and behavior in marketing and branding. By understanding the psychology and cultural significance of color, brands can craft compelling visual identities that resonate with audiences, foster trust, and drive action. Whether through bold statements, subtle cues, or global adaptations, mastering the use of color is essential for standing out in a competitive marketplace.

Chapter 23: Color Therapy: Healing with Hues

Color therapy, also known as chromotherapy, is a holistic practice that uses colors to promote physical, emotional, and mental well-being. This ancient healing technique is based on the idea that colors carry specific energies that can influence our bodies and minds. By understanding how different hues interact with our energy systems, we can harness their power to restore balance and enhance overall health. In this chapter, we delve into the history, principles, and applications of color therapy, exploring how colors can heal and transform.

The Foundations of Color Therapy

Historical Origins

- **Ancient Egypt and Greece**: Egyptians and Greeks used colored gemstones, sunlight, and pigments in healing rituals, believing colors had divine and restorative powers.
- **Ayurveda**: In Indian Ayurvedic practices, colors are linked to the chakras, energy centers in the body, with each chakra resonating with a specific color.
- **Traditional Chinese Medicine**: Ancient Chinese healers associated colors with the elements and organs, using them to balance energy (qi) in the body.

Scientific Basis

- **Light and Energy**: Colors are wavelengths of light, each with unique frequencies and energies that interact with the human body.
- **Impact on the Mind and Body**: Studies show that exposure to specific colors can influence mood, behavior, and even physiological processes like blood pressure and heart rate.

The Psychological and Physiological Effects of Colors
Each color carries unique properties that can affect the body and mind in different ways.
Red

- **Properties**: Stimulates energy, vitality, and circulation.
- **Uses**:
    - Increases physical energy and motivation.
    - Aids in treating fatigue or low blood pressure.
- **Cautions**: Excessive exposure may cause restlessness or anxiety.

Orange

- **Properties**: Boosts creativity, enthusiasm, and digestion.
- **Uses**:
    - Alleviates depression and emotional stagnation.
    - Stimulates appetite and metabolism.
- **Cautions**: Overuse can be overwhelming for sensitive individuals.

Yellow

- **Properties**: Enhances mental clarity, focus, and positivity.
- **Uses**:
    - Improves concentration and decision-making.
    - Supports digestive health and nervous system balance.
- **Cautions**: Too much yellow can lead to irritability or mental fatigue.

Green

- **Properties**: Promotes balance, harmony, and healing.
- **Uses**:
    - Reduces stress and fosters emotional calm.
    - Aids in heart health and immune system function.
- **Cautions**: Generally safe; overuse may feel stagnant or dull.

Blue

- **Properties**: Calms the mind, reduces inflammation, and promotes relaxation.
- **Uses**:
    - Eases anxiety, insomnia, and high blood pressure.
    - Helps in treating throat and respiratory issues.

- **Cautions**: Overexposure may cause feelings of sadness or coldness.

Purple

- **Properties**: Encourages spiritual growth, creativity, and introspection.
- **Uses**:
    - Supports meditation and intuitive practices.
    - Aids in treating migraines and nervous disorders.
- **Cautions**: Excessive use may feel overly introspective or isolating.

White

- **Properties**: Symbolizes purity and cleansing.
- **Uses**:
    - Clears mental clutter and promotes new beginnings.
    - Balances the entire energy system.
- **Cautions**: Too much white can feel sterile or isolating.

Black

- **Properties**: Represents grounding and protection.
- **Uses**:
    - Provides a sense of security and introspection.
    - Helps release negative emotions or energy.
- **Cautions**: Overuse can feel heavy or oppressive.

The Chakras and Their Colors in Color Therapy
Color therapy often aligns with the seven chakras, each associated with a specific color and area of physical and emotional well-being.

1. **Root Chakra (Red):**
   ◦ Location: Base of the spine.
   ◦ Function: Stability, security, and survival instincts.
   ◦ Healing: Red light or objects strengthen grounding and vitality.
2. **Sacral Chakra (Orange):**
   ◦ Location: Lower abdomen.
   ◦ Function: Creativity, sexuality, and emotional balance.
   ◦ Healing: Orange enhances joy, intimacy, and creative expression.
3. **Solar Plexus Chakra (Yellow):**
   ◦ Location: Upper abdomen.
   ◦ Function: Confidence, willpower, and digestion.
   ◦ Healing: Yellow boosts self-esteem and mental clarity.
4. **Heart Chakra (Green):**
   ◦ Location: Center of the chest.
   ◦ Function: Love, compassion, and healing.
   ◦ Healing: Green fosters emotional balance and physical healing.
5. **Throat Chakra (Blue):**
   ◦ Location: Throat.
   ◦ Function: Communication and self-expression.
   ◦ Healing: Blue supports clear speech and calmness.
6. **Third Eye Chakra (Indigo):**
   ◦ Location: Between the eyebrows.
   ◦ Function: Intuition, insight, and imagination.
   ◦ Healing: Indigo aids in meditation and inner vision.
7. **Crown Chakra (Violet):**
   ◦ Location: Top of the head.
   ◦ Function: Spirituality, connection, and enlightenment.
   ◦ Healing: Violet supports spiritual growth and transcendence.

Techniques and Tools in Color Therapy
Light Therapy

- Uses colored light or filters to target specific areas of the body.
- Often used in conjunction with other therapies for conditions like Seasonal Affective Disorder (SAD) or skin issues.

Visualization

- Involves imagining colors during meditation to balance energy or reduce stress.
- Example: Visualizing green for healing or blue for relaxation.

Color Breathing

- Focuses on "breathing in" the energy of a color to align with a desired emotional or physical state.

Color Baths

- Adding colored bath salts or lighting to water enhances relaxation and therapeutic effects.

Crystals and Gemstones

- Incorporating colored crystals like amethyst, citrine, or emerald aligns energy with their corresponding colors.

Wardrobe and Surroundings

- Wearing or surrounding oneself with specific colors to reinforce desired energies throughout the day.

Practical Applications of Color Therapy
At Home

- **Room Design**:
    - Use green in living rooms to promote harmony.
    - Choose blue for bedrooms to encourage restful sleep.
- **Lighting**:
    - Install colored bulbs or smart lighting to adjust hues for mood enhancement.

At Work

- **Productivity**:
    - Yellow in workspaces fosters focus and creativity.
- **Stress Reduction**:
    - Incorporate plants or green accents to create a calming environment.

In Wellness Centers

- **Therapeutic Rooms**:
    - Blue and purple are common in meditation or yoga spaces.
    - Warm tones like orange are used in creative workshops.

Scientific Evidence and Limitations
Evidence

- Studies have shown that color impacts mood, behavior, and even physiological processes.
- Light therapy is widely recognized for treating conditions like SAD and sleep disorders.

Limitations

- Color therapy is complementary and should not replace medical treatment.
- Responses to color are subjective and vary between individuals and cultures.

The Future of Color Therapy
Technology Integration

- Wearable devices that emit specific colored light for health benefits.
- Virtual reality environments that use color to enhance mood and relaxation.

Incorporating Neuroscience

- Advances in neuroscience could provide deeper insights into how colors interact with brain activity.

Sustainability in Color Choices

- Eco-friendly color applications using natural dyes and sustainable lighting solutions.

Conclusion: Embracing the Healing Power of Color

Color therapy offers a simple yet profound way to enhance well-being by aligning the energies of specific hues with our physical and emotional needs. By understanding the unique properties of colors and their effects on our bodies and minds, we can incorporate chromotherapy into our daily lives to foster balance, vitality, and harmony. Whether through light, visualization, or intentional design, the healing power of color provides a holistic path to wellness.

Part 5: Advanced Insights into the Emotional Language of Colors

Chapter 24: Cultural Nuances and Their Influence on Color Perception

Colors hold profound significance across cultures, symbolizing everything from emotions and values to societal norms and religious beliefs. However, their meanings and interpretations vary widely around the world, shaped by history, geography, and tradition. This chapter explores the cultural nuances of color perception, examining how societies assign meaning to colors, how these interpretations influence behavior, and how global brands navigate these differences in a connected world.

The Cultural Lens of Color Perception

Colors do not inherently carry meaning; their interpretations are shaped by cultural contexts, historical associations, and collective experiences.

The Subjectivity of Color

- **Context-Dependent Meaning**: A single color can symbolize vastly different things depending on the culture. For example:
    - White symbolizes purity in Western cultures but is associated with mourning in many Eastern traditions.
    - Red represents luck in China, but in Western contexts, it often conveys passion or danger.
- **Personal vs. Collective Interpretations**: While individuals may have unique emotional responses to colors, cultural norms often guide collective symbolism.

Historical Influences

- **Natural Resources**: The availability of pigments, like the indigo plant in India or cochineal red in Central America, shaped the significance of certain colors.
- **Colonial and Trade Histories**: The introduction of foreign dyes and pigments influenced local color symbolism, such as the European association of purple with royalty due to its rarity and cost.

Religious and Mythological Roots

- Many color meanings are deeply tied to religious or spiritual beliefs:
    - Gold is associated with divinity and immortality in Hinduism.
    - Green symbolizes paradise and renewal in Islam.

Color Symbolism Across Cultures
Red

- **China**: Symbolizes luck, prosperity, and happiness. Used extensively during festivals and weddings.
- **Western Cultures**: Represents love, passion, and danger. Commonly associated with Valentine's Day and warnings.
- **India**: Worn by brides as a symbol of fertility and purity.
- **Africa**: Represents mourning and death in some regions.

Blue

- **Western Cultures**: Associated with trust, stability, and calmness. Frequently used in corporate branding.
- **Middle East**: Symbolizes protection and spirituality. Seen in talismans like the "evil eye."
- **China**: Associated with immortality and the heavens.
- **Latin America**: Linked to religious devotion, particularly to the Virgin Mary.

Green

- **Islamic Cultures**: Represents paradise, renewal, and life. Widely seen in religious contexts and flags.
- **Western Cultures**: Associated with nature, growth, and environmentalism.
- **China**: Historically avoided in some contexts, as a green hat can signify infidelity.
- **Ireland**: Strongly tied to national identity, St. Patrick's Day, and luck.

Yellow

- **China**: Traditionally associated with the emperor and royalty. Represents honor and prosperity.
- **Western Cultures**: Symbolizes happiness and caution. Used for smiley faces and warning signs.
- **India**: Sacred in Hinduism, representing knowledge and learning.

- **Latin America**: Linked to wealth but also associated with mourning in some regions.

White

- **Western Cultures**: Represents purity, innocence, and weddings.
- **Eastern Cultures**: Associated with death, funerals, and the afterlife.
- **Africa**: Symbolizes spirituality and purity in some traditions.
- **Japan**: Represents purity and simplicity, often used in ceremonial contexts.

Black

- **Western Cultures**: Conveys elegance, sophistication, and mourning.
- **African Cultures**: Represents maturity, strength, and spiritual power.
- **Japan**: Used in formal settings but also associated with mystery and misfortune.
- **Middle East**: Symbolizes rebirth and mourning, depending on the context.

Gold

- **Western Cultures**: Represents wealth, luxury, and achievement.
- **China and India**: Symbolizes prosperity, divinity, and good fortune.
- **Middle East**: Associated with elegance and cultural heritage.

The Influence of Geography on Color Perception
Tropical Regions

- Bright and vibrant colors are often celebrated, reflecting the natural environment of vivid flowers, fruits, and sunlight.

Arid and Desert Regions

- Earth tones, such as browns and golds, dominate, inspired by the surrounding landscapes.

Cold Climates

- Darker, muted colors like navy, gray, and black are favored for their practicality and warmth.

Urban Environments

- Neutral tones like black, white, and gray are popular for their modern and minimalist appeal.

Color Perception in Modern Globalization
Adapting Branding for Global Markets

- **Coca-Cola**: Red, a symbol of luck in China, helped the brand integrate seamlessly into the market.
- **Starbucks**: Green, signifying growth and renewal, aligns with global eco-conscious trends while resonating with multiple cultures.
- **McDonald's**: The golden arches leverage yellow's global associations with cheerfulness, adapted to local aesthetics.

Cultural Missteps

- **Pepsi in Southeast Asia**: Changed its vending machines from deep "royal blue" to "light blue," a color associated with mourning in the region.
- **United Airlines**: Once distributed white carnations to passengers in Hong Kong, unaware that white flowers are a symbol of death in Chinese culture.

Cross-Cultural Synergies

- Some colors transcend cultural boundaries, like blue for trust and green for nature, making them safe choices for global brands.

The Role of Color in Rituals and Celebrations
Weddings

- **Western Cultures**: White dresses symbolize purity.
- **India**: Brides wear red or gold, symbolizing fertility and prosperity.
- **Japan**: Brides often wear white kimonos for the ceremony, followed by colorful attire for the reception.

Funerals

- **Western Cultures**: Black clothing signifies mourning and respect.
- **China and India**: White is worn to honor the deceased and signify peace.
- **Mexico**: During Día de los Muertos, bright colors like orange and purple celebrate the memory of loved ones.

Festivals

- **Holi (India)**: Explodes with colors like pink, yellow, and green, celebrating joy and renewal.
- **Chinese New Year**: Dominated by red and gold, symbolizing prosperity and good luck.
- **Carnival (Brazil)**: Features bold, vibrant colors reflecting joy and cultural pride.

Navigating Cultural Nuances in Color Perception
Key Considerations for Designers and Marketers

1. **Research Cultural Contexts**:
   - Understand the historical and symbolic meanings of colors in your target region.
2. **Test Audience Reactions**:
   - Conduct focus groups or surveys to ensure colors resonate positively.
3. **Avoid Assumptions**:
   - Recognize that color meanings may vary even within a single country or demographic group.

Creating Inclusive Color Palettes

- Combine culturally significant colors with neutral tones to appeal to diverse audiences.
- Use adaptable designs that can be localized for different markets.

The Future of Color in a Multicultural World
Technology and Color Adaptation

- Artificial intelligence is enabling personalized marketing that tailors color schemes to individual preferences and cultural contexts.

Sustainability and Eco-Conscious Design

- Natural, earth-based tones are becoming globally popular as eco-consciousness rises.

Celebrating Diversity

- Designers and brands are increasingly incorporating diverse cultural influences, resulting in richer, more inclusive color palettes.

Conclusion: The Power of Cultural Nuances in Color
Understanding cultural nuances in color perception is essential for effective communication, design, and branding in a globalized world. Colors transcend their visual properties to embody history, spirituality, and emotion, connecting people to their cultural identities. By appreciating and respecting these nuances, we can create designs and messages that resonate deeply across cultures, fostering understanding and collaboration in an interconnected world.

Chapter 25: Personalizing Your Color Palette: Unlocking Your Emotional Harmony

Colors have a profound impact on our emotions, energy levels, and sense of self. By curating a personalized color palette, you can align your surroundings, wardrobe, and creative endeavors with your emotional needs and personal expression. This chapter explores the principles of crafting a personalized color palette, offering insights into how specific colors influence mood and how to choose hues that resonate with your individuality and life goals.

The Power of a Personalized Color Palette

Why Personalization Matters

- **Emotional Alignment**: Colors influence how you feel, think, and act. A personalized palette ensures that the colors you surround yourself with uplift and support you emotionally.
- **Authentic Expression**: Your color choices reflect your personality, tastes, and aspirations, helping you communicate who you are without words.
- **Harmonious Living**: A well-curated palette brings cohesion to your wardrobe, home, and creative projects, creating a sense of balance and clarity.

The Science of Color Preferences

- Studies suggest that color preferences are influenced by:
  - **Cultural Background**: Colors associated with positive experiences in your culture tend to be preferred.
  - **Personal Experiences**: Childhood memories, milestones, and emotional associations shape your relationship with certain colors.
  - **Personality Traits**: Introverts may prefer cool, muted tones, while extroverts often gravitate toward bright, bold hues.

Steps to Discovering Your Personal Color Palette
Step 1: Reflect on Your Emotional Needs

- Ask yourself:
    - Which colors make me feel energized and alive?
    - Which colors help me relax and feel at peace?
    - Are there colors that I avoid? Why?
- Create a color journal where you note your reactions to different hues in various settings.

Step 2: Identify Your Signature Colors

- Observe the colors you're naturally drawn to in clothing, decor, and art.
- Take note of recurring themes in your favorite items, such as:
    - **Warm Colors**: Red, orange, yellow for energy and enthusiasm.
    - **Cool Colors**: Blue, green, purple for calmness and introspection.
    - **Neutral Colors**: White, black, gray, brown for simplicity and stability.

Step 3: Align Colors with Your Goals

- Choose colors that support your current goals:
    - **Boost Confidence**: Incorporate red or gold into your wardrobe.
    - **Encourage Creativity**: Use orange and turquoise in your workspace.
    - **Promote Relaxation**: Add soft blues and greens to your bedroom.

Step 4: Consider Your Skin Tone and Features

- Understanding how colors interact with your skin tone, hair, and eyes can guide choices that enhance your appearance.
    - **Warm Skin Tones**: Earthy colors like mustard, olive, and coral are flattering.
    - **Cool Skin Tones**: Jewel tones like emerald, sapphire, and lavender work well.
    - **Neutral Skin Tones**: Versatile shades like beige, charcoal, and soft pastels suit you best.

Step 5: Test and Experiment

- Experiment with swatches, outfits, and decor to see how colors affect your mood and appearance.
- Use online tools or apps that generate color palettes from images or themes that inspire you.

Building Your Personal Color Palette
Core Palette

- Select 3–5 foundational colors that reflect your personality and provide versatility. These are often neutrals or universally flattering tones.
    - Examples:
        - **Minimalist Core**: White, gray, taupe, black, navy.
        - **Vibrant Core**: Red, yellow, teal, coral, emerald.

Accent Colors

- Add 2–3 secondary colors that bring energy or contrast to your core palette.
    - Examples:
        - **Soft Palette**: Blush pink, sage green, powder blue.
        - **Bold Palette**: Fuchsia, orange, royal blue.

Seasonal Variations

- Adjust your palette to reflect the seasons, ensuring variety and freshness.
    - **Spring/Summer**: Bright pastels, floral tones.
    - **Fall/Winter**: Deep jewel tones, earthy neutrals.

Applying Your Personalized Palette to Your Life
Wardrobe

- Build a capsule wardrobe using your core palette for versatility, with accents for variety.
- Use color strategically:
    - **Work Attire**: Navy, gray, or black convey professionalism.
    - **Casual Wear**: Earth tones or denim blues for a relaxed look.
    - **Special Occasions**: Jewel tones or metallics for elegance.

Home Decor

- **Living Areas**:
    - Use your core palette for walls and larger furniture.
    - Incorporate accent colors in cushions, rugs, or artwork.
- **Bedrooms**:
    - Soft, calming colors like lavender or sage promote relaxation.
- **Workspaces**:
    - Bright and energetic hues like yellow or turquoise enhance focus and creativity.

Creative Projects

- Align your palette with your artistic or professional identity. For example:
    - A writer might choose colors that inspire introspection, such as deep blues and purples.
    - A graphic designer might opt for bold, contrasting colors that evoke excitement and attention.

Adapting Your Palette for Emotional Shifts

Life changes and emotional shifts may prompt adjustments to your color preferences. Here's how to adapt your palette to match your evolving needs:

Stressful Times

- Prioritize calming colors like green, blue, or soft gray to create a sanctuary-like environment.
- Avoid overly stimulating colors like bright red or neon yellow.

Exciting Changes

- Incorporate vibrant accents, such as coral, fuchsia, or electric blue, to reflect your enthusiasm and energy.

Reflective Periods

- Use earthy tones like brown, rust, or olive to ground yourself and encourage introspection.

The Role of Color in Emotional Harmony

Colors have the power to balance your emotions and energy, fostering a sense of harmony.

Balancing Energy

- If you feel overactive, introduce cool tones like blue or lavender to create calm.
- If you lack motivation, add energizing colors like orange or red.

Creating Mood Zones

- Designate areas in your home or workspace with specific colors to support different activities:
    - **Meditation Corner**: Shades of green or violet for tranquility.
    - **Creative Space**: Yellow and turquoise to spark ideas.

Tools for Crafting Your Palette
Apps and Software

- **Coolors**: Generates custom palettes based on your preferences.
- **Adobe Color**: Allows you to create palettes using color theory principles.

Physical Tools

- Use paint swatches, fabric samples, or colored pencils to visualize your palette in real life.

Inspiration Sources

- Nature: Observe landscapes, flowers, and skies for harmonious combinations.
- Art: Study works by your favorite artists to discover appealing palettes.

Common Mistakes and How to Avoid Them

- **Overloading with Colors**: Too many colors can feel chaotic. Stick to a core palette with a few accents.
- **Ignoring Lighting**: Colors look different in various lighting conditions. Test your palette in natural and artificial light.
- **Choosing Trend-Driven Colors**: Trends come and go. Focus on timeless hues that resonate with you personally.

Conclusion: Embracing Your Unique Palette

Personalizing your color palette is a journey of self-discovery, helping you unlock emotional harmony and express your true self. By understanding the power of color and its impact on your mood, appearance, and environment, you can create a life infused with beauty, balance, and meaning. Whether you're choosing a wardrobe, decorating a home, or planning a creative project, your personalized palette is a reflection of your individuality and a tool for living authentically.

Appendices

Appendix A: A Complete Guide to Color Symbolism in Different Cultures

Colors carry deep meanings in cultures worldwide, influencing traditions, emotions, and behavior. While the symbolism of colors is universal in some respects, many interpretations are unique to specific cultures, shaped by history, geography, religion, and social norms. This guide provides a comprehensive exploration of color symbolism across cultures, offering valuable insights for understanding and using colors effectively in cross-cultural contexts.

Red: Passion, Luck, and Power

- **China:**
  - Symbolizes luck, prosperity, and happiness.
  - Used in weddings, festivals, and traditional garments.
- **India:**
  - Represents purity, fertility, and marital bliss.
  - Brides traditionally wear red during weddings.
- **Western Cultures:**
  - Associated with love, passion, and danger.
  - Widely used for Valentine's Day and warning signs.
- **Africa:**
  - Represents life and death in some cultures.
  - Used in rituals to symbolize strength or mourning.
- **Japan:**
  - Signifies life and vitality, often seen in traditional ceremonies.

Blue: Trust, Spirituality, and Protection

- **Western Cultures:**
  - Represents trust, calmness, and stability.
  - Common in corporate branding and uniforms.
- **Middle East:**
  - Symbolizes protection, often linked to the "evil eye."
  - Associated with spirituality and peace.
- **China:**
  - Seen as a color of immortality and advancement.
  - Often used in art to depict the heavens.

- **Latin America:**
    - ◦ Represents religious devotion, particularly to the Virgin Mary.
- **India:**
    - ◦ Associated with Krishna, representing divine love and compassion.

Green: Nature, Renewal, and Prosperity

- **Islamic Cultures:**
    - ◦ Considered sacred, symbolizing paradise and renewal.
    - ◦ Used in religious decorations and flags.
- **Western Cultures:**
    - ◦ Represents nature, environmentalism, and growth.
    - ◦ Associated with luck, especially in Ireland.
- **China:**
    - ◦ Traditionally linked to fertility but also avoided in certain contexts (e.g., "wearing a green hat" implies infidelity).
- **Africa:**
    - ◦ Represents life, health, and abundance.
    - ◦ Common in rituals and clothing symbolizing agricultural prosperity.
- **Japan:**
    - ◦ Conveys energy, youth, and vitality, often used in modern design.

Yellow: Happiness, Wisdom, and Caution

- **China:**
    - ◦ Historically associated with emperors and royalty.
    - ◦ Represents honor, wealth, and power.
- **India:**
    - ◦ Sacred in Hinduism, symbolizing learning and knowledge.
    - ◦ Common in religious ceremonies and festivals.
- **Western Cultures:**
    - ◦ Represents happiness, cheerfulness, and caution.
    - ◦ Used in warning signs and marketing to grab attention.
- **Latin America:**
    - ◦ Associated with wealth, but also mourning in some regions.
- **Japan:**
    - ◦ Symbolizes courage and honor, particularly in historical contexts.

White: Purity, Peace, and Mourning

- **Western Cultures:**
  - Associated with purity, innocence, and weddings.
  - Widely used in healthcare settings to signify cleanliness.
- **Eastern Cultures:**
  - Represents death, mourning, and the afterlife.
  - Commonly worn at funerals in countries like China and India.
- **Japan:**
  - Conveys simplicity, purity, and spiritual significance.
- **Africa:**
  - Represents spirituality and purity in rituals.
  - Often used in celebrations for new beginnings.
- **Middle East:**
  - Symbolizes peace and reverence, often worn during religious practices.

Black: Elegance, Mystery, and Mourning

- **Western Cultures:**
  - Associated with sophistication, elegance, and formality.
  - Widely used in mourning and funerals.
- **Africa:**
  - Represents maturity, strength, and ancestral connection.
  - Used in spiritual rituals and ceremonies.
- **Japan:**
  - Linked to formality and mystery.
  - Associated with strength and perseverance, but also misfortune.
- **Middle East:**
  - Symbolizes rebirth and mourning, depending on the context.
- **China:**
  - Represents water, winter, and the unknown in traditional beliefs.

Purple: Royalty, Spirituality, and Creativity

- **Western Cultures:**
    - ◦ Historically associated with royalty and wealth.
    - ◦ Represents creativity, spirituality, and luxury in modern contexts.
- **India:**
    - ◦ Linked to spirituality and mysticism.
    - ◦ Common in religious practices and rituals.
- **China:**
    - ◦ Symbolizes divinity and immortality.
    - ◦ Seen in art and architecture with spiritual themes.
- **Africa:**
    - ◦ Represents wealth and status in some regions.
    - ◦ Used in ceremonial attire and regal symbols.
- **Japan:**
    - ◦ Conveys nobility, power, and elegance.

Orange: Energy, Warmth, and Creativity

- **Western Cultures:**
    - ◦ Represents energy, enthusiasm, and warmth.
    - ◦ Often used in marketing to convey vibrancy and fun.
- **India:**
    - ◦ Sacred in Hinduism, representing purity and devotion.
    - ◦ Commonly seen in monks' robes and religious symbols.
- **Japan:**
    - ◦ Symbolizes courage, strength, and love.
- **Latin America:**
    - ◦ Associated with energy and passion, often used in celebrations.
- **Middle East:**
    - ◦ Evokes feelings of warmth and creativity, often used in art and textiles.

Brown: Stability, Grounding, and Simplicity

- **Western Cultures:**
    - Represents reliability, simplicity, and grounding.
    - Commonly associated with nature and rustic lifestyles.
- **Africa:**
    - Linked to the earth, fertility, and life.
    - Frequently used in cultural expressions and traditional crafts.
- **Japan:**
    - Symbolizes humility and simplicity, often used in traditional design.
- **Latin America:**
    - Represents connection to land and heritage.
    - Seen in indigenous clothing and art.

Gold: Wealth, Divinity, and Success

- **Western Cultures:**
    - Associated with luxury, achievement, and prosperity.
    - Widely used in awards, trophies, and celebratory decor.
- **China and India:**
    - Symbolizes prosperity, divinity, and good fortune.
    - Often used in weddings, festivals, and religious ceremonies.
- **Middle East:**
    - Represents elegance and spiritual power.
- **Africa:**
    - Symbolizes wealth and high status, often used in jewelry and art.

Navigating Cultural Sensitivities with Color
Global Considerations

- Understand the target culture's history and values to avoid misinterpretation.
- Conduct research or consult local experts when designing products, advertisements, or experiences for specific regions.

Adapting Color for Multicultural Audiences

- Use versatile color schemes that resonate across cultures (e.g., blue for trust and green for growth).
- Balance culturally significant colors with neutral tones to create inclusivity.

Recognizing Regional Variations

- Within countries, regional differences may influence how colors are perceived. For example:
    - In India, saffron (orange) is sacred across the nation, but other shades may have varied meanings in different regions.

Conclusion: Harnessing the Power of Color Across Cultures
Color symbolism is a rich and dynamic field, deeply intertwined with cultural identities and traditions. By understanding how colors are perceived and used worldwide, we can navigate cross-cultural communication with sensitivity and creativity. Whether designing for global markets, personal expression, or creative projects, appreciating these cultural nuances allows us to use color as a bridge for connection and understanding.

Appendix B: Exercises and Resources for Practicing Color Awareness

Color awareness is a skill that enhances your ability to perceive, interpret, and use colors effectively in various aspects of life. From designing harmonious spaces to selecting impactful palettes, practicing color awareness fosters creativity, emotional intelligence, and cultural sensitivity. This appendix offers hands-on exercises and curated resources to help you deepen your understanding of color theory, symbolism, and practical applications.

Exercises to Build Color Awareness

1. Daily Color Journaling

- **Objective**: Observe and reflect on how colors affect your mood and environment.
- **Steps**:
    1. Keep a journal to record the dominant colors you encounter each day.
    2. Note the settings (home, nature, work) and your emotional reactions to these colors.
    3. Reflect on patterns—do certain colors consistently uplift or calm you?
- **Benefit**: Builds mindfulness about the impact of color in your daily life.

2. Color Wheel Exploration

- **Objective**: Familiarize yourself with the relationships between colors.
- **Steps**:
    1. Print or create a color wheel.
    2. Practice identifying primary, secondary, and tertiary colors.
    3. Experiment with creating complementary, analogous, and triadic color schemes.
- **Benefit**: Enhances your ability to choose harmonious color combinations.

3. Create a Personal Mood Board

- **Objective**: Curate a visual representation of colors that resonate with your personality or goals.
- **Steps**:
    1. Collect images, fabric swatches, or paint samples in your favorite colors.
    2. Organize them on a physical or digital board.
    3. Use the board to identify trends in your preferences (e.g., vibrant tones, earthy neutrals).
- **Benefit**: Helps you develop a personal color palette for your wardrobe, home, or creative projects.

4. Color in Nature

- **Objective**: Observe how colors occur naturally and how they interact.
- **Steps**:
    1. Spend time outdoors in diverse environments (gardens, forests, urban landscapes).
    2. Take photos or sketch the colors you notice.
    3. Analyze the harmony and contrast in these natural palettes.
- **Benefit**: Inspires fresh ideas and fosters an appreciation for organic color combinations.

5. Cultural Color Research

- **Objective**: Understand how colors are perceived in different cultural contexts.
- **Steps**:
    1. Choose a culture and research the meanings of its traditional colors.
    2. Create a visual chart or write a summary of your findings.
    3. Compare and contrast these meanings with your own cultural associations.
- **Benefit**: Builds cross-cultural awareness and sensitivity in color usage.

6. Experiment with Lighting

- **Objective**: Learn how lighting affects color perception.
- **Steps**:
    1. Place a colored object in different lighting conditions (natural light, warm bulbs, cool bulbs).
    2. Observe how the color changes in tone and intensity.
    3. Document your observations to identify which lighting enhances specific colors.
- **Benefit**: Improves your ability to design spaces and images with optimal lighting.

7. Emotional Color Mapping

- **Objective**: Connect colors with emotions and experiences.
- **Steps**:
    1. Reflect on a significant memory or mood.
    2. Assign colors that represent those feelings.
    3. Create a visual representation (drawing, painting, or collage) to capture the emotional landscape.
- **Benefit**: Deepens your understanding of the emotional impact of colors.

8. Color Matching Challenge

- **Objective**: Train your eye to distinguish subtle variations in color.
- **Steps**:
    1. Gather paint swatches or use a digital tool to create a color gradient.
    2. Try to match the colors in the gradient precisely using art supplies or digital editing tools.
    3. Evaluate how well your matches align with the original tones.
- **Benefit**: Sharpens your attention to detail and accuracy in color perception.

Resources for Developing Color Awareness
Books

1. **"Interaction of Color" by Josef Albers**:
    - Explores the relativity and interaction of colors.
    - Includes exercises to improve color sensitivity.
2. **"Color: A Natural History of the Palette" by Victoria Finlay**:
    - A fascinating journey through the history and cultural significance of colors.
3. **"The Secret Lives of Color" by Kassia St. Clair**:
    - Delves into the history, symbolism, and psychology of individual colors.

Online Tools and Apps

1. **Adobe Color (color.adobe.com)**:
    - A digital tool for creating and analyzing color palettes.
    - Includes features for exploring harmony rules and themes.
2. **Coolors (coolors.co)**:
    - A simple and intuitive palette generator.
    - Useful for experimenting with different color combinations.
3. **Pigment by ShapeFactory (pigment.shapefactory.co)**:
    - Allows you to create aesthetically pleasing gradients and palettes.

Workshops and Courses

1. **Skillshare**:
    - Offers courses on color theory, graphic design, and painting.
    - Recommended Course: *"Color Theory Basics: A Beginner's Guide to Color Harmony."*
2. **Coursera**:
    - Provides academic-level courses on design and color psychology.
    - Recommended Course: *"Introduction to Graphic Design" by California Institute of the Arts.*
3. **Local Art Classes**:
    - Check community centers or art schools for workshops focused on painting, design, or interior decorating.

Physical Resources

1. **Color Swatch Books**:
    - Purchase swatch books from brands like Pantone or paint companies to explore professional color systems.
2. **Colored Pencils or Paint Sets**:
    - Experiment with blending and creating custom shades using art supplies.

Websites and Blogs

1. **Design Seeds (design-seeds.com)**:
    - Features color palettes inspired by nature, travel, and daily life.
2. **ColourLovers (colourlovers.com)**:
    - A community-driven platform for sharing and exploring color palettes and patterns.
3. **Canva Color Wheel (canva.com/colors/color-wheel/)**:
    - A beginner-friendly tool for understanding color harmony.

Tips for Incorporating Color Awareness into Daily Life

- **Observe Your Surroundings**: Pay attention to the colors around you and how they make you feel.
- **Experiment with New Palettes**: Step out of your comfort zone and try wearing or decorating with colors you wouldn't normally choose.
- **Share Your Insights**: Discuss color meanings and preferences with friends, family, or colleagues to expand your understanding.

Conclusion: Practicing Color Awareness for Creative Growth

By engaging in these exercises and leveraging the resources provided, you can enhance your ability to perceive and utilize colors with intention and precision. Whether you're a designer, artist, or someone seeking to live more harmoniously, cultivating color awareness will empower you to make choices that resonate emotionally and aesthetically. This practice is not only a creative journey but also a pathway to deeper self-expression and connection with the world around you.

<u>Message from the Author:</u>

I hope you enjoyed this book, I love astrology and knew there was not a book such as this out on the shelf. I love metaphysical items as well. Please check out my other books:

-Life of Government Benefits

-My life of Hell

-My life with Hydrocephalus

-Red Sky

-World Domination:Woman's rule

-World Domination:Woman's Rule 2: The War

-Life and Banishment of Apophis: book 1

-The Kidney Friendly Diet

-The Ultimate Hemp Cookbook

-Creating a Dispensary(legally)

-Cleanliness throughout life: the importance of showering from childhood to adulthood.

-Strong Roots: The Risks of Overcoddling children

-Hemp Horoscopes: Cosmic Insights and Earthly Healing

- Celestial Hemp Navigating the Zodiac: Through the Green Cosmos

-Astrological Hemp: Aligning The Stars with Earth's Ancient Herb

-The Astrological Guide to Hemp: Stars, Signs, and Sacred Leaves

-Green Growth: Innovative Marketing Strategies for your Hemp Products and Dispensary

-Cosmic Cannabis

-Astrological Munchies

-Henry The Hemp

-Zodiacal Roots: The Astrological Soul Of Hemp

- **Green Constellations: Intersection of Hemp and Zodiac**

-Hemp in The Houses: An astrological Adventure Through The Cannabis Galaxy

-Galactic Ganja Guide

Heavenly Hemp

Zodiac Leaves

Doctor Who Astrology

Cannastrology

Stellar Satvias and Cosmic Indicas

<u>Celestial Cannabis: A Zodiac Journey</u>

AstroHerbology: The Sky and The Soil: Volume 1

AstroHerbology:Celestial Cannabis:Volume 2

Cosmic Cannabis Cultivation

The Starry Guide to Herbal Harmony: Volume 1

The Starry Guide to Herbal Harmony: Cannabis Universe: Volume 2

Yugioh Astrology: Astrological Guide to Deck, Duels and more

Nightmare Mansion: Echoes of The Abyss

Nightmare Mansion 2: Legacy of Shadows

Nightmare Mansion 3: Shadows of the Forgotten

Nightmare Mansion 4: Echoes of the Damned

The Life and Banishment of Apophis: Book 2

Nightmare Mansion: Halls of Despair

<u>Healing with Herb: Cannabis and Hydrocephalus</u>

<u>Planetary Pot: Aligning with Astrological Herbs: Volume 1</u>

Fast Track to Freedom: 30 Days to Financial Independence Using AI, Assets, and Agile Hustles

<u>Cosmic Hemp Pathways</u>

How to Become Financially Free in 30 Days: 10,000 Paths to Prosperity

Zodiacal Herbage: Astrological Insights: Volume 1

Nightmare Mansion: Whispers in the Walls

The Daleks Invade Atlantis

Henry the hemp and Hydrocephalus

10X The Kidney Friendly Diet

Cannabis Universe: Adult coloring book

Hemp Astrology: The Healing Power of the Stars

Zodiacal Herbage: Astrological Insights: Cannabis Universe: Volume 2

<u>Planetary Pot: Aligning with Astrological Herbs: Cannabis Universes: Volume 2</u>

Doctor Who Meets the Replicators and SG-1: The Ultimate Battle for Survival

Nightmare Mansion: Curse of the Blood Moon

<u>The Celestial Stoner: A Guide to the Zodiac</u>

Cosmic Pleasures: Sex Toy Astrology for Every Sign

Hydrocephalus Astrology: Navigating the Stars and Healing Waters

Lapis and the Mischievous Chocolate Bar

Celestial Positions: Sexual Astrology for Every Sign

Apophis's Shadow Work Journal: **:** A Journey of Self-Discovery and Healing

Kinky Cosmos: Sexual Kink Astrology for Every Sign

Digital Cosmos: The Astrological Digimon Compendium

Stellar Seeds: The Cosmic Guide to Growing with Astrology

Apophis's Daily Gratitude Journal

Cat Astrology: Feline Mysteries of the Cosmos

The Cosmic Kama Sutra: An Astrological Guide to Sexual Positions

**Unleash Your Potential: A Guided Journal Powered by AI Insights
Whispers of the Enchanted Grove**

Cosmic Pleasures: An Astrological Guide to Sexual Kinks
369, 12 Manifestation Journal
Whisper of the nocturne journal(blank journal for writing or drawing)
The Boogey Book
Locked In Reflection: A Chastity Journey Through Locktober
Generating Wealth Quickly:
How to Generate $100,000 in 24 Hours
Star Magic: Harness the Power of the Universe
The Flatulence Chronicles: A Fart Journal for Self-Discovery
The Doctor and The Death Moth
Seize the Day: A Personal Seizure Tracking Journal
The Ultimate Boogeyman Safari: A Journey into the Boogie World and Beyond
**Whispers of Samhain: 1,000 Spells of Love, Luck, and Lunar Magic: Samhain Spell Book
Apophis's guides:
Witch's Spellbook Crafting Guide for Halloween
<u>Frost & Flame: The Enchanted Yule Grimoire of 1000 Winter Spells</u>
<u>The Ultimate Boogey Goo Guide & Spooky Activities for Halloween Fun</u>**
Harmony of the Scales: A Libra's Spellcraft for Balance and Beauty
The Enchanted Advent: 36 Days of Christmas Wonders

Nightmare Mansion: The Labyrinth of Screams
Harvest of Enchantment: 1,000 Spells of Gratitude, Love, and Fortune for Thanksgiving
The Boogey Chronicles: A Journal of Nightly Encounters and Shadowy Secrets
The 12 Days of Financial Freedom: A Step-by-Step Christmas Countdown to Transform Your Finances
Sigil of the Eternal Spiral Blank Journal
A Christmas Feast: Timeless Recipes for Every Meal
Holiday Stress-Free Solutions: A Survival Guide to Thriving During the Festive Season
Yu-Gi-Oh! Holiday Gifting Mastery: The Ultimate Guide for Fans and Newcomers Alike
Holiday Harmony: A Hydrocephalus Survival Guide for the Festive Season
Celestial Craft: The Witch's Almanac for 2025 – A Cosmic Guide to Manifestations, Moons, and Mystical Events
Doctor Who: The Toymaker's Winter Wonderland
Tulsa King Unveiled: A Thrilling Guide to Stallone's Mafia Masterpiece
Pendulum Craft: A Complete Guide to Crafting and Using Personalized Divination Tools
Nightmare Mansion: Santa's Eternal Eve
Starlight Noel: A Cosmic Journey through Christmas Mysteries
The Dark Architect: Unlocking the Blueprint of Existence

Surviving the Embrace: The Ultimate Guide to Encounters with The Hugging Molly

The Enchanted Codex: Secrets of the Craft for Witches, Wiccans, and Pagans

Harvest of Gratitude: A Complete Thanksgiving Guide

Yuletide Essentials: A Complete Guide to an Authentic and Magical Christmas

Celestial Smokes: A Cosmic Guide to Cigars and Astrology

Living in Balance: A Comprehensive Survival Guide to Thriving with Diabetes Insipidus

Cosmic Symbiosis: The Venom Zodiac Chronicles

The Cursed Paw of Ambition

Cosmic Symbiosis: The Astrological Venom Journal

Celestial Wonders Unfold: A Stargazer's Guide to the Cosmos (2024-2029)

The Ultimate Black Friday Prepper's Guide: Mastering Shopping Strategies and Savings

Cosmic Sales: The Astrological Guide to Black Friday Shopping

Legends of the Corn Mother and Other Harvest Myths

Whispers of the Harvest: The Corn Mother's Journal

The Evergreen Spellbook

The Doctor Meets the Boogeyman

The White Witch of Rose Hall's SpellBook

The Gingerbread Golem's Shadow: A Study in Sweet Darkness

The Gingerbread Golem Codex: An Academic Exploration of Sweet Myths

The Gingerbread Golem Grimoire: Sweet Magicks and Spells for the Festive Witch

The Curse of the Gingerbread Golem

10-minute Christmas Crafts for kids

<u>Christmas Crisis Solutions: The Ultimate Last-Minute Survival Guide</u>

Gingerbread Golem Recipes: Holiday Treats with a Magical Twist

The Infinite Key: Unlocking Mystical Secrets of the Ages

Enchanted Yule: A Wiccan and Pagan Guide to a Magical and Memorable Season

Dinosaurs of Power: Unlocking Ancient Magick

Astro-Dinos: The Cosmic Guide to Prehistoric Wisdom

Gallifrey's Yule Logs: A Festive Doctor Who Cookbook

The Dino Grimoire: Secrets of Prehistoric Magick

The Gift They Never Knew They Needed

The Gingerbread Golem's Culinary Alchemy: Enchanting Recipes for a Sweetly Dark Feast

A Time Lord Christmas: Holiday Adventures with the Doctor

Krampusproofing Your Home: Defensive Strategies for Yule

Silent Frights: A Collection of Christmas Creepypastas to Chill Your Bones

Santa Raptor's Jolly Carnage: A Dino-Claus Christmas Tale

Prehistoric Palettes: A Dino Wicca Coloring Journey

The Christmas Wishkeeper Chronicles

The Starlight Sleigh: A Holiday Journey

Elf Secrets: The True Magic of the North Pole

Candy Cane Conjurations

Cooking with Kids: Recipes Under 20 Minutes
Doctor Who: The TARDIS Confiscation
The Anxiety First Aid Kit: Quick Tools to Calm Your Mind
Frosty Whispers: A Winter's Tale
The Infinite Key: Unlocking the Secrets to Prosperity, Resilience, and Purpose
The Grasping Void: Why You'll Regret This Purchase
Astrology for Busy Bees: Star Signs Simplified
The Instant Focus Formula: Cut Through the Noise
If you want solar for your home go here: https://www.harborsolar.live/apophisenterprises/

Get Some Tarot cards: https://www.makeplayingcards.com/sell/apophis-occult-shop

Get some shirts: https://www.bonfire.com/store/apophis-shirt-emporium/

<u>**Instagrams:**</u>
@apophis_enterprises,
@apophisbookemporium,
@apophisscardshop
Twitter: @apophisenterpr1
Tiktok:@apophisenterprise
Youtube: @sg1fan23477, @FiresideRetreatKingdom
Hive: @sg1fan23477
CheeLee: @SG1fan23477

Podcast: Apophis Chat Zone: https://open.spotify.com/show/5zXbr-CLEV2xzCp8ybrfHsk?si=fb4d4fdbdce44dec

Newsletter: https://apophiss-newsletter-27c897.beehiiv.com/

If you want to support me or see posts of other projects that I have come over to: **buymeacof-fee.com/mpetchinskg**

I post there daily several times a day

Get your Dinowicca or Christmas themed digital products, especially Santa Raptor songs and other musics. Here: **https://sg1fan23477.gumroad.com**

Apophis Yuletide Digital has not only digital Christmas items, but it will have all things with Dinowicca as well as other Digital products.